CHRISTIANS IN THE ARENA

This is Samuel's only book re: Christianity
He's not in Wikepedia

Important Notes:
2021 - This book/writer appears to be
VERY RIGHT WING politically
VERY CONSERVATIVE christian .. a Christian 166, 60
but I can learn, maybe understand, even respect, agree often
-- but uneasy, guarded -- published 2006
....
Samuel's best known books are about nature's
"Nature Never Stops Talking" - where God is not
mentioned.
He is big time into music .. a variety

* I have concluded this is Samuel J.
speaking his views, opinions as a
Bible believing Christian.
He makes one/me think, pray, read God's word & live
my Christian life - Valuing, understanding as a
United States citizen.

CHRISTIANS IN THE ARENA

✦ ✦ ✦

Stepping Into the Arenas of Leadership, Influence and Political Controversy

Samuel J. Alibrando

Tsaba House
Reedley, CA

Cover and text design by Bookwrights
Senior editor, Jodie Nazaroff
Author photo by Andrea Lundgren

Published by
Tsaba House
2252 12th Street, Reedley, California 93654
Visit our website at www.TsabaHouse.com

Printed in the United States of America

Revised and expanded second edition: 2006

Library of Congress Cataloging-in-Publication Data

Alibrando, Samuel J., 1953-
Christians in the arena : stepping into the arenas of leadership, influence, and political controversy / by Samuel J. Alibrando. — 2nd ed.
p. cm.
Includes index.
ISBN-13: 978-1-933853-46-8 (pbk. : alk. paper)
ISBN-10: 1-933853-46-8 (pbk. : alk. paper)
1. Christian life. 2. Conduct of life. I. Title.
BV4501.3.A44 2006
277.3'083—dc22

2006013086

DEDICATION

As we grow up, we have many models and people to imitate but only one father.

I idolized my dad as a child but became a rebellious teen, running away from home at barely age 17. I continued on my own path, hitch-hiking cross country and traveling to England alone. My ways were grievous to my father. Although he may have been unsure of how to respond, what to do or say, his love did not waver; but I did not know this.

It was not until I was in my mid 30's that I began to believe my dad really loved me. Still, we found little to discuss when talking long distance on the phone.

In my 40's we finally began discussing business matters, sharing personal feelings, and our relationships with God, the Bible, and family members. Our relationship became closer than ever before and this has been consistent for years now. I also have had the great opportunity to discover his lifestyle of helping others. He continually gets up in the morning and gets cracking for veterans, widows, and friends. He will attack any injustice that has the misfortune of coming to his doorstep or those he cares about. Even now in his 70's he badgers those in authority seeking to deprive ill veterans of rightful services they deserve.

To have an earthly father that loves my heavenly Father is great. To anticipate my dad being my "brother" for eternity and the opportunity to enjoy him more on the "other side" is a wonderful hope. To be in my 50's and still have a dad and one that I genuinely look up to is a rare treasure.

I dedicate this book to him. Thanks Dad.

✦ ✦ ✦

Acknowledgment

In the 1970's Dr. Murray Norris was still alive and doing the impossible on a nearly daily basis. He was recognized as an inspiring person with a gift for communicating how to change circumstances. He encouraged others to believe they could do more. He always had a sparkle in his eye as though to say, "If I can do it, I know you could do it way better." He was humble that way. Even though he seemed to be frequently struggling financially, he kept going. He wrote, published papers, brainstormed, managed affairs, and did speaking engagements internationally.

In 1979, Dr. Norris literally urged and inspired me to write the early version of this book.

✦ ✦ ✦

Contents

✦ ✦ ✦

Introduction

It is my hope that you will not find this book to be merely one man's opinion, but rather a man presenting scripture, which begins in Chapter 3. Originally I was going to provide just the scripture references, but too often readers keep reading the text without looking them up or they may not have a Bible readily available. Most importantly, it is the rich meaning of scripture itself that has center stage here.

Years ago, 1978 to be precise, I felt moved to present a series of topics at a community center in the small town of Solvang, CA. At the time I was a youth director for a church in Santa Ynez. The topics were not polite dinner conversation but I felt clear on my leading. To my shock the people who seemed most angry with me were not those I would have expected at age 26. They were church people. I was confused and spent much time shut in with the Bible for days praying. At the conclusion of that time I realized what I was doing was not only a scriptural directive but that somehow I had overlooked it for years and possibly, so had the church. I began looking for a book on why our founding fathers could ignore Romans 13 about obeying governmental authority. All I could find were books on the fact that they were Christian, not the scriptural reasons they used to sway a largely Christian population to rebel against the British Crown.

I simply began my own research. It was Murray Norris, mentioned here and in the introduction of another book of mine "Nature Never Stops Talking", who encouraged me to write. God rest his soul.

In this book, you will find the scriptures separate from my text and in a different font. The reference is given at the bottom of the scripture with the version quoted. My words are just that, my words, but the scripture is of the utmost authority.

Permit me to comment on the adjective "Christian". I do not mean one who believes in God. So do the demons. I do not mean one who attends church. Again, history and our own eyes know that church attendance does not a Christian make. Quoting scripture had even been used by Satan to tempt Jesus. I also am not including or excluding any specific denomination.

By "Christian" I mean a person whose belief in the grace of God through Jesus results in a submitted life evidenced by the fruits of the Spirit in Galatians chapter 5, a dependence on God and His wisdom, an ever-increasing reflection of the character of Jesus Christ in them . . . LOVE. God IS Love.

The heart of God's plan and the heart of Christianity is love. Love is too important to be misunderstood. We need to see and experience the true love of God so that we are not abandoned to dictionaries, intellectualizing, semantics, or popular usage.

The Bible goes on about love in 1 Corinthians 13:

...love does not rejoice in unrighteousness, but rejoices with the truth;

Heaven forbid that I should not continue growing and learning in my life. For that reason I can comfortably say that with time I may disagree with a point or two in this book. Don't be surprised. I have said the same thing from pulpits. How ignorant could I be to tell people that they can trust me as much as scripture? How naïve could I be to assume that what I say or have printed is 100% right. After 20 years of marriage, I still can't convince my wife that I'm always right.

I want to keep learning. However, I hope to enlighten you with scriptures and meanings therein which you may have previously overlooked as I had.

Anything that you don't agree with, ignore it; yeah, ignore it. But whatever strikes you as absolutely true, especially if it reveals the need for change—embrace it fully.

I have another important point about this book. I have enjoyed books that "kept me company" or that were comfortable conversations. This book is short and frankly, I hope it keeps your attention. It is short because action requires FEWER words. An auto manual isn't read for pleasure but as a guide. It is to be used and implemented to fix problems with your car; likewise here.

Meditate on the words here. Consider this as impacting you personally. Mark up this book for your future reference. Write personal notes in the margins, PLEASE. Take the words, especially the scriptures, right off the pages and into your mind and chew on it until it settles into your heart. From your heart, allow the quality of your character to bring forth a life of conviction and live out what you understand and truly believe to be right.

Prologue

I am delighted so many folks around the world have embraced my last book, *Nature Never Stops Talking -The Wonderful Ingenuity of Nature*, as a resource for noticing the evidence of design that is right in front of them. The glorious genius evidenced in the technology, interdependence, and the seamless tapestry we call nature remains an overwhelming testimony always.

Those with an agenda are more interested in trying to make Intelligent Design a religious controversy. In order to quash the clear rationality that Intelligent Design is more sensible than random accidents, tricky tactics must replace facts. Proving theories with experiments is easy for the Intelligent Design argument. Proving theories for explosions, accidents, and random chance as the finest genius in the universe have no experiments to back up such nonsense. After 150 years, evolutionary theory largely still has no hard evidence.

Those readers and fans who appreciated my non-religious approach to a subject so universally loved as nature, will find this book a completely different format. With my presentation of science and nature there were no scriptures, no religion, and God was not even mentioned.

In this book the scripture, rather than the scientific method, is my standard of proof. However, there are several things this book has in common with *Nature Never Stops Talking*. As in *Nature Never Stops Talking*, I encourage readers to not necessarily believe me, but believe what I point to as a reference. In *Nature Never Stops Talking* I point to nature and provable experiments. In *Christians in the Arena* I point to the Bible. "Go look for yourself" is my echoed theme. There may be less who completely believe the Bible than believe nature, but it is Bible-believing people to whom I address this book.

I am directly stating points that many will take to task. I am glad. My only request is that you take the scriptures to task—not me. If you feel I have twisted the scripture's meaning or ignored some large message in the Word, you should be able to confirm that from the Word; not your opinion, not your denomination, not your feeling, not history, not something terrible you saw, heard, or read.

My challenge to all is simply this: "Is this what the Bible is teaching?" This is the basis of discussion in this book.

I have taken some time to discuss the true origins of the United States. I did this primarily for the young people who do not realize many of the things older folks assume everyone knows; the country used to be a Bible-believing, openly praying, godly nation and it was always legal, until lately.

There is something else that may almost appear contradictory but it is all Bible. For most of the book I make the case that Christians ought to speak out and make the voice of morality known; I then take an entire chapter from the Old Testament using Daniel as a model citizen. He said almost nothing in a dark land that had their own gods, yet he was continually promoted to very high positions WITHOUT compromising his walk with our God. He is a great example of integrity and holding the standard. The point with the book of Daniel is that preaching the truth is far less important than walking the walk. We need to do this no matter how dark our generation becomes. But what if they asked Daniel to rule in government? What would he say? Would he say he had no opinion or was busy? Daniel served in his capacity in that form of government; but in America, we are asked to vote, we are invited to serve in public positions, we are welcome to run for public office, we are welcome to express our contrary opinions under freedom of speech, which adversaries of God use vigilantly.

This book is a call to vigilance and to obedience according to His call as described throughout scripture. It is not a patriotic hurrah for our Christian heritage but instead a carefully focused presentation of scripture commanding us to love others by NOT hiding the truth about the difference between right and wrong.

We are like kings—none of us are forbidden to rule. It is a hard and challenging task but God commands us to overcome sin in ourselves and in the arenas in which we are able to exert influence.

CHAPTER ONE

✦ ✦ ✦

Church and State

Some Christians talk about the separation of church and state as though this doctrine was of divine origin. They cannot be separated. Just try and separate values and law. Try to separate philosophy from how you govern any nation. Try and separate religion from governing any people.

Church and state are INSEPARABLE, just as laws and values are inseparable.

If we remove godliness from government, if we remove godliness from our schools, something ungodly and evil fills that vacuum.

Of course, there is always a philosophy in government. You can call it a "philosophy", a "religion", or a "set of values", whatever it is ... it will be for good or for evil; that belief system will inevitably influence decisions.

In England, the state church was determined by the religion of the monarchy before the discovery of America. The king's favoritism of one denomination sometimes subjected other denominations to unfair treatment. The king's church became the "state church". The "state church" denomination would pay no taxes while the denominations not enjoying the same favor might be taxed, restricted, or even persecuted.

The original intent of "Separation of Church and State" is a far cry from its current interpretation and I can easily prove it. However, to satisfy curiosity about what the founding fathers intended is my reason for offering this explanation. Our nation's founding fathers sought to avoid this partiality by separating church and state from unjust treatment of particular denominations. NEVER DID OUR FOUNDERS INTEND TO ESTABLISH A GOVERNMENT DEVOID OF GOD. There is abundant evidence on this point. From the establishment of our government to today, sessions of Congress and the Senate are opened with prayer. Who prays? The appointed Chaplin paid with tax dollars since the inception of our nation. They prayed over the meetings arguing how to form this nation. This being the custom is one clear indicator that our nation always intended to seek the favor and guidance of God in all government matters—not expel Him. To expel God is quite the opposite.

It is obvious they sought His blessing, His guidance, and did frequently refer to His Holy Word. As a matter of historical fact, the entire establishment of America was largely a Christian and spiritual vision in deference to the Holy Bible as the supreme tangible source of law, value, and government. You don't have to believe me; read the Declaration of Independence, read the Constitution, or read your own state constitution. All 50 state constitutions honorably refer to God. I will provide some quotes in this book. Read The Christian History of the Constitution of the United States, Vol. I: Christian Self-Government by Verna M. Hall, published by The Foundation for American Christian Education at www.face.net.

This book is not written to prove that historical vision, or learn the traditions set down by our forefathers. Nor is this writing about the re-writing of our history to hide our true heritage from American students. I will make reference to these concepts. However, this author's objective is to discern what God wants us to do NOW, based on what scripture teaches.

It is still important to recognize that we have been brainwashed because we do not take time to pursue the facts. There is nothing sacred about separation of church and state. On the contrary, it is an evil deception that intercepts Christianity while permitting every other religion and philosophy free access to all government and public affairs.

This single notion of idealized separation of church and state has kept thousands, if not millions of Christians from becoming community leaders. Due to the misunderstanding of this separation between the community and the church, too many are serving only within the walls of their church. This idea that one cannot publicly serve God while serving the community is a farce. What a tragedy, to make God sit at the back of the bus, ignored as though not present in all open forums. He is suddenly uninvited.

Just as sad is the idea that to wholeheartedly serve God, one must serve strictly and exclusively within church functions.

Separating personal religious preference in governing is a historically correct interpretation of our form of government for more than 200 years. This is a mighty far cry from current objective of diligently removing godliness and Christianity from all aspects of public life.

It is a perversion to take God and the Bible out of government, *especially* the American government. It is a perversion to take God and the Bible out of anything. Yet, removing God and the Bible from government, education, science, psychology, history and our society at large is exactly what has been accepted by Americans, both Christian and non-Christian, as a normal thing.

Do you think Satan is interested in politics?

Is not a government devoid of God, a clear tool of Satan; if not a tool of Satan then, anti-God forces; if not anti-God forces then, at the very least strong convictions that God is unimportant or the Bible meaningless clutter? If politics, legislation, and activities on the civil, state, and federal levels were of no spiritual consequence, certainly Satan would not get involved. However, look at so many of the activities of our government and see the works of evil purposes against Christian principles and institutions. This is of no service to God, individuals or the community or America. It is practically, if not literally, against the intent of the Constitution.

THE BATTLE OF CONSPIRACIES

Don't think anyone is paranoid when they suggest that the ungodly have an agenda to outlaw Christian values. Likewise, don't blame politicians for accusing Christians of having a conspiracy to implement Judeo-Christian ethics. True Christians should have that agenda. Why should anyone ignore his own values and embrace those values he or she disagrees with or considers wrong?

There are lying politicians that pretend they are Christian to get the Christian vote. These folks are of no value to the kingdom of God or the citizens they serve. Why? Because God really is smart, God really is right, His laws and values are truly the very best for all people everywhere. Why? Because God really understands what He personally created. Real, practicing believers with integrity using God's values on behalf of the community is what America could use, by many millions. Tell me how does it benefit a community or nation to outlaw the posting of the Ten Commandments?

Let's examine how "oppressive" the Ten Commandments are.

1. Love God.
2. Don't make false idols to worship.
3. Don't use God's name in vain [oppressing anyone so far?]
4. Rest on the 7th day of the week.
5. Honor your father and mother [contrary to some school curriculums].
6. Do not murder.
7. Do no commit adultery [schools teach the use of condoms, not self-control].
8. Do not steal.
9. Do not lie.
10. Be content with what you have and don't covet your neighbor's stuff.

What if everyone in our nation abided by all ten? Everyone; no stealing, no murder, everyone obeyed and honored mom and dad, everybody stayed home and relaxed once a week, everyone considered God as the most important person to honor and respect. Imagine no one lying. If people cussed, they wouldn't use the Lord's name;

no sexual cheating on husband or wife; everyone strives to improve, without envying others; the rich being content with what they already have; everybody loving God. If our whole country was like that, and DID OBEY the Ten Commandments what kind of nation would this be? Would this create a great nation or would it be oppressive? This is the vision of the majority or the early settlers and the founding fathers, and for most of two centuries there has been little disagreement about that.

Why are millions so totally committed to convincing our generation that these are wrong principles to the point of making it illegal to post them on public school walls? Even more alarming, why are millions of Christians unwilling to stand up for these same principles and commandments as true and right; as our true heritage?

There is a contest. There are opposing conspiracies. There will ultimately be one and only one winner. These are not compatible philosophies.

Understand that nothing remains stagnant. We are either gaining ground or losing ground. Things do not remain the same. This is true in most of life. Christians must put their values into the laws or the ungodly will put *their* values into law. Either the ungodly use the laws to force their ungodly values on Christians and all citizens or Christians will use the laws to force godly values on Christians and all citizens, PERIOD. It is that simple. It is a contest either way. Don't believe that it isn't.

If we politely nod our head and say, "I don't want to fight about it", then those that are willing to fight for what they believe will prevail. Then, they will fight against your Christian values and if again you say, "I don't want to fight about it", your Christian values will become criminal in the land that was once a Christian nation. And that, my friend, has already happened on many matters.

This is where we are now. Still, most Christians say, "I don't want to fight about it." So what is next? Santa is in, Jesus is out. The Easter bunny is in, resurrected Christ is out. Witchcraft and Ouija boards are harmless fun while children must be legally protected from the Ten Commandments, the Bible and Jesus Christ. All religions are welcome but Christianity is restricted.

The enemy [spiritual forces] has already celebrated the defeat of Christianity in America. We are no longer defending our territory. We have already lost it. Like the Jews conquered by the Romans, we can do our traditional stuff but under Roman rule. Churches are non-profit corporations that by law can only maintain their non-profit status if they refrain from political activity. Doesn't this strike you as at the very least, an interesting restriction? Our churches are governed by the "Romans".

However, unlike a conquered people, we still have citizenship equal to the "Romans". We are even welcome to rule if we desire. We are still welcome to object, even if the objection is ignored. Yes, it is now too late for a defensive strategy. Even in the ranks of the church, sin is embraced and the Bible is interpreted to conform to politically correct ideas. The only strategy that makes sense at this stage is an uprising; but who will go?

"I don't want to fight about it" is how we got here and it will get even worse unless we do fight about it. Obviously, many Christians have given up their Christian values. Maybe our values are far less like God's than we care to admit.

But God owns victory, it is His property. And not only America, but the whole earth is the Lord's.

The horse is prepared for the day of battle,
But victory belongs to the LORD.

Proverbs 21:31 (NASB)

The earth is the LORD'S, and all it contains,
The world, and those who dwell in it.

Psalms 24:1 (NASB)

CHAPTER TWO

✦ ✦ ✦

Rewriting American History

MOSES AND THE TEN COMMANDMENTS

Below are some good reasons to take your children to Washington D.C. before the ACLU (American Civil Liberties Union) or the AUSCS (Americans United for the Separation of Church and State) succeed in erasing all clues of our real heritage.

As you walk up the steps of the building which houses the U.S. Supreme Court you can see near the top of the building a row of the world's law givers. Each one is facing the one in the center who is facing forward with a full frontal view. That is Moses.

In our American history, the Bible has been our basis for law and government. Our founding fathers reviewed other governments, lawgivers, and philosophers as well. They were far more educated than most graduates with 7 year degrees today. As I said, at the center of these figures on the Supreme Court building is Moses and he is holding the Ten Commandments—that's right, the Ten Commandments from the Bible; the Ten Commandments from Mount Sinai written by the finger of God Himself. It's the same Ten Commandments banned from school rooms by new interpretations of law but still today, you and/or your children can see the true foundation of our heritage displayed for all.

Ironic, isn't it? The very foundation of our laws in America is exactly what is outlawed in so many places.

As you enter the Supreme Court courtroom the two huge oak doors have the Ten Commandments engraved on the lower portion of each door.

As you sit inside the courtroom you can see on the wall right above where the Supreme Court judges sit a display of the Ten Commandments.

There are Bible verses etched in stone all over the Federal Buildings and Monuments throughout Washington, D.C.

James Madison, the fourth president, known as "The Father of Our Constitution" made the following statement: "We have staked the whole of all our political institutions upon the capacity of mankind for self-government, upon the capacity of each and all of us to govern ourselves, to control ourselves, to sustain ourselves according to the Ten Commandments of God."

Patrick Henry, that patriot and Founding Father of our country said:

"It cannot be emphasized too strongly or too often that this great nation was founded not by religionists but by Christians, not on religions but on the Gospel of Jesus Christ."

Our U.S. government was not founded on the principle that all religions are equal but that the Bible is true. It is upon these truths our government and laws have been established. All around the world different religions have a major influence on their own nation. America was founded by families—no, an entire people—who declared biblical Christianity as the truest values worth embracing.

This is not just for practicality, but to invoke the favor of the living God. This was as important as not invoking God's anger by worshipping any other god or false religion. On this premise our country went from a small colonized area to the dominant world power in a mere 200 years among nations established thousands of years earlier.

That is why every session of Congress begins with a prayer by a paid preacher, whose salary has been paid by the taxpayer since 1777.

Many Christian traditions have included prayer at many public events such as football games, graduations, and many public functions. It is peculiar that what the majority of Americans are comfortable with continues to be systematically outlawed as wrongful and illegal by a small minority offended by American tradition.

Fifty two of the fifty-five founders of the Constitution were members of the established orthodox churches in the colonies.

Thomas Jefferson worried that the Courts would overstep their authority and instead of interpreting the law would begin making law . . . an oligarchy. ("Oligarchy" means the rule of few over many). I think his fear may be all too real. The majority of Americans believe in God and the Ten Commandments as good. Most consider Christ in Christmas as valid and respectable. Our tolerant attitude toward all people was to respect the rights of minorities, not give minorities the license to rule and *not* respect the rights of the majority.

The very first Supreme Court Justice, John Jay, said: "Americans should select and prefer Christians as their rulers."

REWRITING AMERICAN HISTORY

The rewriting of history is bluntly, a work of deception. It is the disrespectful task of changing facts to be more agreeable with an agenda; in a word "lying". But it is careful lying that has all the makings of conspiracy. It is an intentional effort to make children believe older history was wrong. Eventually no one remembers the previous history, thus, our past is reconstructed—even our origins and the creation of life.

Let me be more direct. There is a conscious, diligent, widespread effort to eliminate all respect for biblical Christianity. Make no mistake about it. I am not a paranoid right wing extremist. I have cringed at mentioning these facts because of the obvious target I paint on myself as "paranoid" or even the more mild "misguided" tag. Christianity and biblical mandates were once as acceptable as good manners here in the United States.

In 1962, my 4th grade teacher in Abington, PA was Mrs. Russell. She would read from the Bible every morning to our class. It was also that very year that such practice was outlawed. It was that year that Mrs. Russell had to stop reading to us. She seemed upset and she explained to us but frankly, it meant very little to me as a 9-year old.

In 1995, 33 years later, I was talking to my own daughter about the history of the United States and the topic of the separation of church and state. It didn't occur to me that Christianity had always been "illegal" in public schools during her lifetime. She had been exposed to the idea that there were aggressive extremists that would sometimes try to force religion into the public places. Her impression was that they were disrespectful of the separation of church and state. Naturally, it had a negative flavor to it and she literally imagined that somehow even the founding fathers desired religion to be apart and away from all facets of public gatherings and activities. Only so-called extremists were acting contrary to the Constitution in my daughter's mind. Of course she would believe that. It is all she heard. So I took it upon myself to add another version to her understanding.

I explained to her that the opposite was true. I told her that if we viewed a timeline of American history from the 15th century to today, that Christianity was not merely embraced in America, but it was the primary influence in our government, laws, and education. I explained that all congressional meetings and meetings of the Senate were opened with prayer, as they still are. I told her that all education, including all of the original colleges including what are now considered Ivy League universities such as Harvard and Yale, were originally established to educate so graduates would know God better so to make Him better known. The Bible was not "tolerated" but central to our educational system for nearly 300 years—older than the official age of the United States. Religious freedom was not to demote God or dishonor Him. God and the Bible have always been revered throughout American history by the majority of the population and its leaders. There is a mere sliver on America's time line where Christianity and the Bible are treated with contempt by the government and the laws. That little sliver of time is a recent occurrence even though to her, it had been all her life.

Naturally, there have always been and always will be religious hypocrites and enemies of the church, but Christian values and the Bible have long been regarded as the American way.

Even the word "religion" was referring to various denominations of Bible-believing churches. As politically incorrect as it may sound, during most of American history, non-Bible believing religions were not considered legitimate in America. Attractive or unattractive, this is our history. For the majority of our history, our prosperity has been publicly considered God's blessing upon us for our efforts to please Him. Ever hear the phrase "God Bless America"? This is why many still give a prayer of thanks for their food—thanks for God's blessing.

Through the centuries most anti-Bible practices stayed in the closet, fearing coming out, due to the overwhelming social norms of America.

This is the true heritage of America. The founding, governing, and maintaining of the United States of America has been largely a pursuit with the conscious and open goal of being pleasing to God and desiring His blessing.

Fifty years ago our children were well protected, but not today. Today, we are made to believe that there is an almost divine wisdom to removing God from all government, laws, education, public events, public displays, and the influence of our children. However, it is OK if our children are exposed to all other religions. It is OK if our children are exposed to fiction and non-fiction where Jesus Christ is represented by serial killers, lunatics, or psychos quoting scripture. It is OK if our children read about folks mocking Jesus Christ, Christianity, and the Bible in serious or comedic ways. Today what American children are supposed to be protected from is any influence of Christianity, Jesus, or the Bible as inspirational, respectfully or with honor.

Today, much of what is on normal TV would have been considered pornography 50 years ago. The things that would have been considered unspeakable 50 years ago are considered acceptable today. Indecent pornography then would have been any imitation of a man and woman together sexually. The acting out of the suggestion was indecent, just as it would be in a church play today. However, 50 years ago no one would have tried selling homosexual interaction because not only was there no market demand for such "entertainment" but it would have been repulsive to most American pornographers at that time. The courts today have been zealous to protect children from the "harmful effects" of the Ten Commandments, Christian influence, intelligent design discussion, or any alternate theories suggesting that evolution may be a weak theory.

Where is our voice? Where is the strength of the moral Americans?

Dear reader, what would the world think if Americans went into the Middle East and tried instituting "religious freedom" by outlawing the Muslim religion? The world would be outraged.

America has turned itself against itself and is calling it "freedom".

If a foreign nation tried to outlaw Christianity in America 50 years ago there would be war. If we do it ourselves by calling it separation of church and state, we call it "religious freedom".

When we read how Herod killed all the Jewish children under age 3 during the time of Jesus, we rightfully consider it a horror. If we pass laws saying mothers can kill their own children and millions do, we call it women's rights.

If our country was overrun by a foreign nation and they ordered the execution of millions of unborn children—what would be the universal response? How unbelievable is it that mothers are literally encouraged to do the same?

There is a perverse work in our nation where we are celebrating disobedience to God and all that is reasonably healthy. It is not sophisticated, it is not modern, it is not liberal, it is not civilized, but it is self-destructive.

We have abandoned our identity as a nation like a rebellious teenager who wants to prove he is not the respectable person his family "forced" him to be while he was growing up.

Our "liberty" has become bondage with the inevitable consequences of bad choices.

We ignore true science to embrace a myth that denies God as creator.

We ignore the values of faithfulness, loyalty, courage, and honesty to embrace the relentless pursuit of self-indulgence and call it our pursuit of happiness.

Finally, we rewrite history in an attempt to erase even a hint of what we once were—a successful experiment of the first and only Christian nation, founded on biblical principles and embracing biblical morality, making us the greatest and most prosperous nation on earth.

STATE CONSTITUTIONS

Like corporations and trusts, every single state has a guiding document. In corporations and trusts there are by-laws. In our states these are called constitutions. No doubt organizations will try to change this history also, but take notice that all 50 state constitutions address God directly; *ALL 50 STATES*. This was no big news 40 years ago but for many today, it is shocking.

Seeking the favor of God, the guidance of God, and the help of God is traditional in America. Expressing gratefulness to God, reverence for God, recognizing Him as Creator, Ruler of the Universe, and Author of Existence are common among official statements in the various state constitutions.

America's founders and even the state founders never intended for there to be a separation of God and state, as it is being misinterpreted today. Their true intentions are undeniably shown by the fact that all 50 states acknowledge God in their state constitutions.

Alabama 1901, Preamble. We the people of the State of Alabama, *invoking the favor and guidance of Almighty God*, do ordain and establish the following Constitution...

Alaska 1956, Preamble. We, the people of Alaska, *grateful to God* and to those who founded our nation and pioneered this great land...

Arizona 1911, Preamble. We, the people of the State of Arizona, *grateful to Almighty God for our liberties*, do ordain this Constitution...

Arkansas 1874, Preamble. We, the people of the State of Arkansas, *grateful to Almighty God* for the privilege of choosing our own form of government...

California 1879, Preamble. We, the People of the State of California, *grateful to Almighty God* for our freedom...

Colorado 1876, Preamble. We, the people of Colorado, *with profound reverence for the Supreme Ruler of the Universe…*

Connecticut 1818, Preamble. The People of Connecticut, *acknowledging with gratitude the good Providence of God* in permitting them to enjoy…

Delaware 1897, Preamble. *Through Divine Goodness all men have, by nature, the rights of worshipping and serving their Creator* according to the dictates of their consciences.

Florida 1885, Preamble. We, the people of the State of Florida, *grateful to Almighty God* for our constitutional liberty establish this Constitution...

Georgia 1777, Preamble. We, the people of Georgia, *relying upon protection and guidance of Almighty God*, do ordain and establish this Constitution...

Hawaii 1959, Preamble. We, the people of Hawaii, *grateful for Divine Guidance* ...establish this Constitution.

Idaho 1889, Preamble. We, the people of the State of Idaho, *grateful to Almighty God for our freedom* to secure its blessings…

Illinois 1870, Preamble. We, the people of the State of Illinois, *grateful to Almighty God for the civil, political and religious liberty which He hath so long permitted us to enjoy and looking to Him for a blessing on our endeavors…*

Indiana 1851, Preamble. We, the People of the State of Indiana, *grateful to Almighty God* for the free exercise of the right to choose our form of government…

Iowa 1857, Preamble. We, the People of the State of Iowa, *grateful to the Supreme Being for the blessings hitherto enjoyed, and feeling our dependence on Him for a continuation of these blessings establish this Constitution.*

Kansas 1859, Preamble. We, the people of Kansas, *grateful to Almighty God for our civil and religious privileges*, establish this Constitution.

Kentucky 1891, Preamble. We, the people of the Commonwealth of Kentucky, *grateful to Almighty God for the civil, political and religious liberties...*

Louisiana 1921, Preamble. We, the people of the State of Louisiana, *grateful to Almighty God for the civil, political and religious liberties we enjoy…*

Maine 1820, Preamble. We the People of Maine, *...acknowledging with grateful hearts the goodness of the Sovereign Ruler of the Universe in affording us an opportunity ...and imploring His aid and direction.*

Maryland 1776, Preamble. We, the people of the state of Maryland, *grateful to Almighty God for our civil and religious liberty...*

Massachusetts 1780, Preamble. We...the people of Massachusetts, acknowledging with grateful hearts, *the goodness of the Great Legislator of the Universe ... in the course of His Providence, an opportunity and devoutly imploring His direction...*

Michigan 1908, Preamble. We, the people of the State of Michigan, *grateful to Almighty God for the blessings of freedom*, establish this Constitution.

Minnesota 1857, Preamble. We, the people of the State of Minnesota, *grateful to God for our civil and religious liberty*, and desiring to perpetuate its blessings…

Mississippi 1890, Preamble. We, the people of Mississippi in convention assembled, *grateful to Almighty God, and invoking His blessing on our work...*

Missouri 1845, Preamble. We, the people of Missouri, *with profound reverence for the Supreme Ruler of the Universe, and grateful for His goodness...* establish this Constitution...

Montana 1889, Preamble. We, the people of Montana, *grateful to Almighty God for the blessings of liberty...*establish this Constitution.

Nebraska 1875, Preamble. We, the people, *grateful to Almighty God for our freedom...*establish this Constitution.

Nevada 1864, Preamble. We the people of the State of Nevada, *grateful to Almighty God for our freedom* establish this Constitution.

New Hampshire 1792, Part I Art. I. Sec. V. Every individual has a natural and unalienable *right to worship God* according to the dictates of his own conscience...

New Jersey 1844, Preamble. We, the people of the State of New Jersey, *grateful to Almighty God for civil and religious liberty which He hath so long permitted us to enjoy, and looking to Him for a blessing on our endeavors...*

New Mexico 1911, Preamble. We, the People of New Mexico, *grateful to Almighty God for the blessings of liberty...*

New York 1846, Preamble. We, the people of the State of New York, *grateful to Almighty God for our freedom,* in order to secure its blessings...

North Carolina 1868, Preamble. We the people of the State of North Carolina, *grateful to Almighty God, the Sovereign Ruler of Nations, for our civil, political, and religious liberties, and acknowledging our dependence upon Him for the continuance of those...*

North Dakota 1889, Preamble. We, the people of North Dakota, *grateful to Almighty God for the blessings of civil and religious liberty,* do ordain...

Ohio 1852, Preamble. We the people of the state of Ohio, *grateful to Almighty God for our freedom, to secure its blessings* and to promote our common...

Oklahoma 1907, Preamble. *Invoking the guidance of Almighty God, in order to secure and perpetuate the blessings of liberty...* establish this Constitution.

Oregon 1857, Bill of Rights, Article I Section 2. All men shall be secure in the *natural right, to worship Almighty God* according to the dictates of their consciences...

Pennsylvania 1776, Preamble. We, the people of Pennsylvania, *grate-*

ful to Almighty God for the blessings of civil and religious liberty, and humbly invoking His guidance…

Rhode Island 1842, Preamble. We the People of the State of Rhode Island *grateful to Almighty God for the civil and religious liberty which He hath so long permitted us to enjoy, and looking to Him for a blessing…*

South Carolina, 1778, Preamble. We, the people of the State of South Carolina, *grateful to God for our liberties*, do ordain and establish this Constitution.

South Dakota 1889, Preamble. We, the people of South Dakota, *grateful to Almighty God for our civil and religious liberties...* establish this…

Tennessee 1796, Art. XI.III. *That all men have a natural and indefeasible right to worship Almighty God according to the dictates of their conscience...*

Texas 1845, Preamble. We, the People of the Republic of Texas, *acknowledging, with gratitude, the grace and beneficence of God…*

Utah 1896, Preamble. *Grateful to Almighty God for life and liberty, we establish this Constitution.*

Vermont 1777, Preamble. Whereas all government ought to....enable the individuals who compose it to enjoy their natural rights, *and other blessings which the Author of Existence has bestowed on man…*

Virginia 1776, Bill of Rights, XVI. *Religion, or the Duty which we owe our Creator can be directed only by Reason ... and that it is the mutual duty of all to practice Christian Forbearance, Love and Charity towards each other.*

Washington 1889, Preamble. We the People of the State of Washington, *grateful to the Supreme Ruler of the Universe for our liberties*, do ordain this Constitution...

West Virginia 1872, Preamble. *Since, through Divine Providence,* we enjoy the blessings of civil, political, and religious liberty, we, the people of West Virginia, *reaffirm our faith in and constant reliance upon God.*

Wisconsin 1848, Preamble. We, the people of Wisconsin, *grateful to Almighty God for our freedom*, domestic tranquility…

Wyoming 1890, Preamble. We, the people of the State of Wyoming, *grateful to God for our civil, political, and religious liberties* establish this Constitution...

These declarations are overwhelming evidence of the legal normalcy of praying to God, honoring God, seeking to please God openly, officially, publicly, in government and frankly, in every level of government.

After reviewing acknowledgments of God from all 50 state constitutions, is one not faced with the obvious prospect that none of our state's constitutions were breaking the law nor had they any intention of breaking the law? Although we are right to protect minorities in America, it was never intended that the minority would rule the majority.

A minority is abusing laws protecting their rights and steamrolling over the rights of the majority. The courts have been systematically and increasingly restricting biblical morality and all the benefits that adhering to those biblical morals have given to America. That which once was the inspiration, guide, and backbone of our country is becoming outlawed. The "invited guests" at the table of American tradition are insisting they should be more than guests and that our American traditions are offensive to them and should be stopped.

All 50 states, 100%, did not misunderstand our Constitution or the desire of our founding fathers by expressing honor and thanks to God. No, the evidence is very clear that all these state constitutions are in compliance with the desire of our founding fathers, the laws of the land, and the will of the people. America, throughout most of its history, has pursued God's guidance and blessing. "God Bless America" has a genuinely long history in the U.S.

These state constitutions prove that calling out to God publicly was not only perfectly legal, but the norm in our American culture.

CHAPTER THREE

✦ ✦ ✦

Laws and Values

LAWS PROCLAIM VALUE

Law is a guide. This is why we need Christian legislators. This is why we need Christian governors, Christian Congressmen, Christian Supreme Court judges, State, County and local judges, Senators, mayors, councilmen, policemen and representatives at every level.

The laws of a nation reflect and influence the values of that people. For example, if there are no laws to protect family unity and many laws with large fines to protect the environment, it becomes clear that the family is of minor importance to that society but the environment is of greater importance.

PENALTIES PROCLAIM VALUE

While the laws of a nation reflect and influence the values of their people, the penalties indicate more precisely the degree of importance. The range goes from no enforcement to death penalty. On one end, it isn't important, on the other, society is saying they will not tolerate certain behavior.

For instance, where I live, a parking ticket requires a certain fine but parking in a handicapped zone gets a much steeper fine. This is the community's way of saying "it is less tolerable to deprive a handicapped person from parking than someone who is not handicapped."

As in the Bible, a town or a nation, the penalty for a crime reveals just how serious the crime is *to that society*—whether it is a small fine or capital punishment.

Look at the laws carefully and you will see the values they seek to protect. In our nation, a government of elected officials, a government "of the people," the laws reflect our own values and what is important to us. Do our laws reflect your values? If not, what are you going to do about it?

ENFORCEMENT PROCLAIMS VALUE

While laws reflect and influence citizens' values, enforcement reflects the current attitude toward those values. No one cares or expects some old laws to be enforced anymore. It was once criminal to swear in the presence of women and children. Tried the movies lately? I hear cussing at restaurants frequently. It has become part of our culture. Those values were important when the law was originally written but are no longer important, even if the law is still on the books. Adultery is still illegal in many states. However, this law is rarely enforced anymore. This reveals how a society's values change both laws and the enforcement of those laws. Enforcement goes where there is the most pressure from the community. Does the practice of enforcement in your community reflect your values?

GOD'S LAWS PROCLAIM HIS VALUES

We question God's severity each time we see God's decree for stoning someone to death in Exodus, Deuteronomy, or Leviticus. We should look to see *what is so valuable to God that He wants to protect it so zealously.* His laws reflect His values.

If certain things seem too severe to you, that's OK. It simply shows your values are somewhat different from God's. That means you still have more to learn from God. When you have nothing more to learn from God; know for sure you are deceived.

Believers who enter politics represent the people since they are there by popular vote. More importantly, true Christians must represent their God on earth. So there is no deception, be clear about your standards on issues if you run for an office or position so when you are voted in you, your voters, and those who voted against you already know your clear intentions. You must utilize everything you can muster to incorporate God's standards into the lives of those you represent.

I am not describing conquering the ungodly. Is it wrong to provide guidance to protect the innocent? Shouldn't leaders seek to educate the young and naive? Don't we want leaders that will help relieve the oppressed and to reward right conduct? This is the duty of all Christians and they should be the best leaders. They should genuinely care about ALL the people.

Consider this: a man or woman who is ungodly gets voted into office based on their popular beliefs of pro-abortion, keep all religious activities out of schools, gay marriage, etc. You do realize, don't you, that some of these things they may have said just to get the vote. They may go to church in front of cameras. They may lie for votes. Do you think they will lie after getting in office? Do you think they really care about the groups they pretend to defend or are they doing that to keep a job? They may hide their agenda while you put your cards on the table and this may cost you the position. Don't give up. You really care about all the people. They don't. The truth, like a slippery piece of wood in a creek, always manages to slip out and pop up for everyone to see.

Christians must put their values into the laws, or the ungodly will use the laws to force their values on Christians. It is that simple.

GOOD LAWS AND BAD PEOPLE = BAD GOVERNMENT

Even good laws in the hands of the immoral can be a tool of Satan.

> But we know that the Law is good, if one uses it lawfully
>
> **1 Timothy 1:8 (NASB)**

If there are no laws to protect the family unity, it is obvious that the family is of little importance to that society.

It is necessary not only to have good laws passed, but to have them righteously upheld from the police to the juries. Christians with the privilege of governing do not have God's permission to ever walk away from this responsibility. We are to see that good laws are rightly carried out. Otherwise, un-enforced good laws become a joke.

The spirit of law cannot continue without men and women with a lawful spirit. Evil men will *always* pervert the law if given a chance.

Satan is infamous for quoting God and His Word. Why would Satan willingly quote scripture? He is an expert at twisting the meaning of what was intended. Twisting turns the truth into deception. This is constantly done in nearly every court in our land today as the technicality of the words of law prevails over the spirit of the law. This is done in so many arenas today it is depressing.

Christians must do more than merely stand by while good laws are perverted in courts of justice, in city halls and on the streets.

We, the Christians in America, are a sleeping giant. There is no gang, no organized crime, and no ungodly government that can oppose "the armies of the living God". However, Christians have just handed over their power because we have been too busy with other things in our life. Be careful that what you call "quality of life" is not a euphemism for disobedience to God. I don't know your particular situation, but God does.

When Christians leave the creation, enactment, or enforcement of laws to ungodly men how can we expect justice from these evil men? I am not talking about someone's religion. When I say ungodly, I mean against God. Unfortunately, I know too many self-proclaimed Christians that I consider ungodly. But even well-meaning people can wreak havoc in our land. Anything contrary to God's law is evil—anything. People that are against God's laws are by scriptural definition, "evil". They don't even understand true justice. I am not exaggerating or making a careless statement! Look at Solomon's words:

Evil men do not understand justice
but those who seek the Lord understand all things.

Proverbs 28:5 (NASB)

Scripturally it is God's people who are most qualified for political leadership, judgeships, and for responsible decisions. By yielding these offices to others we are inviting oppression on ourselves, our families and our fellow man. If we elect the ungodly we can expect ungodly government; simple enough? If we elect religious hypocrites we should expect ungodly government. These are simple rules. Apple trees make apples. Orange trees make oranges. Ungodliness makes ungodliness.

If a family wanted a puppy but only had a cat, would they pray for their cat to have puppies? Truly, is this not as logical as electing non-believers to office and praying for righteous law and government?

We cannot expect godliness from the ungodly any more than we should expect puppies from cats.

> It is we who must pray and repent. ...my people who are called by My name humble themselves and pray, and seek My face and turn from their wicked ways, then I will hear from heaven, will forgive their sin, and will heal their land.
>
> **2 Chronicles 7:14 (NASB)**

Notice we must pray, but we must also repent and turn from our own wicked ways . . . THEN we get results from God. That is His promise.

CHAPTER FOUR

✦ ✦ ✦

Persecution or Judgement?

RIGHTEOUS PERSECUTION OR GOD'S JUDGEMENT

In light of the obvious apathy and poor stewardship among the majority of Christians in America, would you say the persecution coming to the church is righteous persecution or do you think America feels threatened by the church because it is so holy? Are the ungodly afraid because of the ungodliness being purged from so many churches, towns, and communities nationwide? That would indeed be wonderful but it is not true.

It is sad to admit that most of the persecution coming to the church is because of its uselessness, not its righteousness. Church tax exemption is being threatened because we aren't performing our godly function. God has told His people to minister to the poor and needy. For the bulk of America's history prior to the turn of the 20th century, the church was primarily responsible for all education in America, helping the needy, the widows, and the orphans. Even the unbelievers had to admit the value of the church, even if they disagreed with biblical beliefs. If the church spent its money in a way reflecting the scriptures it would not be primarily on real estate and salaries. The church has turned inward and long abandoned its primary ministries to those that could usually not pay the church back; the true widows, orphans, the poor, and the needy. But the government, through taxation, has picked up this ministry since it was so neglected. The government has also taken over many of the functions of the family, such as care of the elderly, child-care, health-care, and areas of education that properly belong inside the family circle.

Though from New Jersey, I am more familiar with the California public school system. Legally in California, starting in kindergarten, children are to be taught that homosexuality is OK. Of course the instruction is somewhat subtle and is to prevent violence against homosexuals. I agree with the objective of preventing violence, but why in the world can't we teach children that violence is incorrect. Instead of this message, the law is telling children ALL lifestyles are correct and there is no such thing as deviant. I believe very few parents aspire for their child to become homosexual. Why teach it as acceptable? Even worse, why force this on all California children in public education?

Here is a partial list of instruction not taught prior to 1955, but currently being taught to American children in most public schools.

- Sex-education including masturbation, birth-control, and abortion
- Family structure—the normalcy of homosexuality and trans-genderism
- American history WITHOUT God
- Evolution as the only respectable scientific theory for the origin of life and the universe
- One-world government for world peace
- All religions are equal (except for Christianity, which is oppressive)
- All lifestyles are acceptable (except for Christianity which is judgmental)

Before you become outraged, understand something. The church once dominated education. Where family and church have broken down or retreated, the government has stepped in with tax-supported programs.

Too many of our churches are sitting pretty materialistically-- but they are morally putrid. The same can be said for many of the Christian families. Do you feel defensive? Is the divorce rate any different in the church than out of the church?

No wonder a secular government permits churches to continue. All propaganda to defame the church will never injure her as much as our own pettiness, selfishness, and hypocrisy in the public eye. The scandals that have uncovered Christian leaders greedily siphoning thousands of dollars from folks are abundant. The frequent reports of adultery by church leadership are embarrassing but it continues nationwide. How I ache to even mention the scourge of our sins. Propaganda will never ruin us as quickly as our own real sins in the world's eyes and God's.

It is easy to understand why those outside God's family would want to stop tax exemptions for the churches. Why should we have a tax exemption; because we want to enlarge the church building, because we want to increase our membership, because we sing hymns and praises to God? Why should we get tax exemptions? Is it because we are teaching "prosperity" to members by having them give the church money? Isn't "prosperity" the same goal most Americans and every lottery ticket buyer have?

We are no longer the salt of the earth and the light of the world. It seems we love ourselves and our members but point our finger at the "wrong" denominations and the rest of the world.

Although I discuss the sins in the world and government, in this book I want to show scripturally that God's cross hairs are on us, not them.

It is pitiful to see thousands of compromising Christians leaders getting downright angry about possibly losing their tax-exempt status while shrugging their shoulders with "You can't fight city hall" on more important issues. The truth is we can fight city hall about fighting pornography that ruins millions. Who will stop the never-ending push of the ACLU to "protect" the public from Jesus Christ? Is their no outcry at the laws protecting the legality of the murder of unborn children? We seem too politically correct to protest teaching our children volumes of evolution. We are too polite to object to the constant teaching by media, science, laws, and public education that the Bible is absurd. We are too busy to argue with educational publishers deleting our Christian heritage in America with slanted history books.

On the other hand, we see unity to fight "City Hall" when it comes to taking away the tax-exempt status from churches and ministries. I have watched indignant Christian leaders suddenly unite to lead the masses and charge City Hall when money is involved. Oh, this is so grievous.

I really am a positive person and hate to sound cynical. I constantly quote Philippians 4:8 to myself and work at thanking God in all things. But I cannot lie about what I see. It is important that we see our misaligned priorities are too often more focused on money than people. The fruit we see in our own generation should be enough evidence for all to agree something is wrong on a massive scale.

Christians should fight for the innocent and naive and weak with the same zeal that many use only to fight for their tax-exempt status.

Almost everything that Christians should believe from the Bible has been challenged, mocked, and frequently denounced. This happens while there are many great Christian magazines, radio and TV programs, and churches; where is that uprising or reaction to the moral peril of our entire nation?

We are not ignoring the heroes out there, and they are out there. There are those who are active in the communities. There are tremendous individuals who put themselves at risk every day to serve the Lord in saintly ways. They would nod in agreement at this accurate diagnosis regarding the majority of believers in America.

Nevertheless, to speak the truth, uncover lies, and call out to God while sincerely repenting of our own sin is right. Christians are not close to bondage and oppression. We have already crossed the line. We are in bondage and oppression. Think about it.

If you agree with God's Holy Word, you are a virtual outlaw by today's standards. True Bible believers, and this excludes many church attendees, are rebelling against most everything that is politically correct today. Action is not an offensive push for evangelism but now a DEFENSIVE MUST for the real church to even maintain its legal right to influence. Biblical standard holiness is already perceived as a radical minority. To get our country back there must be a confrontational uprising. We are already tagged as a threat to American peace, freedom, and love. Yeah, that's what they say.

Only "women-haters" are against abortion.

Only "homo-phobic, judgmental, prejudiced people" think homosexuality is wrong.

Only "ignorant religious fanatics" refuse to accept the scientific reality of evolution.

Folks, we are called the "minority" in a land once loving the Bible, but today the majority of media and entertainment's slant on us is not flattering.

We are like the Israelites who cried out to God, not because of their loyalty, but because He was their last hope. They found themselves surrounded and outnumbered by enemies.

God really is our only hope. Like the Jews in the book of Esther, there is a growing anger being fanned against us in our own land. Having enemies is nothing new to God's people or God. The only unknown is this: Will we go with the tide of rebellion against God, or will YOU rebel against the rebellion and serve Him?

Most of the following scriptures tell how God delivered Israel, but the cycle starts with Israel rejecting God. There is certain oppression. Then they cry out to God for deliverance. When the cry is desperate and sincere, God comes to their rescue. Then the cycle begins again. God is so merciful to not give up on us and our fickleness altogether.

Notice the sequence of scripture references. This verse is right after the generation who followed Joshua. I am adding italics to focus on Israel continually turning away from their Savior.

Then the Israelites *did evil* in the eyes of the LORD
and served the Baals.

Judges 2:11 (NIV)

The Israelites *did evil* in the eyes of the LORD; they forgot the
LORD their God and served the Baals and the Asherahs.

Judges 3:7 (NIV)

After 8 years in subjection to another king they *cried out to God. God raised up a hero*, Othniel, and delivered them, giving them peace until he died 40 years later.

> And the children of Israel *did evil again* in the sight of the LORD: and the LORD strengthened Eglon the king of Moab against Israel, because they had done evil in the sight of the LORD.
>
> **Judges 3:12 (KJV)**

Time passed. In Judges Chapter 3, verses 14-31, we find that after 18 years under a different king the Israelites cried out to God. God raised up Ehud. Israel had peace for 80 years. Shamgar also saved Israel after Ehud, single-handedly killing 600 Philistines with an ox goad.

> And the children of Israel *again did evil* in the sight of the LORD, when Ehud was dead.
>
> **Judges 4:1 (KJV)**

The Israelites were cruelly oppressed for 20 years and finally cried out to God for help. Deborah, a prophetess, delivered Israel giving it peace for 40 years, according to Judges Chapters 4 and 5; but...

> *Again the Israelites did evil* in the eyes of the LORD, and for seven years he gave them into the hands of the Midianites.
>
> **Judges 6:1 (NIV)**

Israelites tried hiding from their oppressors by living in caves. Several nations bullied them and continually burned their crops. They cried out to God and Gideon was called to deliver Israel. There was another 40 years of peace as seen in Chapters 7 and 8; but again...

> No sooner had Gideon died *than the Israelites again prostituted themselves to the Baals*. They set up Baal-Berith as their god and did not remember the Lord their God, who had

rescued them from the hands of all their enemies on every side.

Judges 8:33-34 (NIV)

Many deliverers were sent because of God's mercy in response to their cries. Every time, once delivered, the redeemed would get relaxed about serving God and then forsake Him...over and over again.

Isn't this true in our own lives? How many military people cry out to God during a battle for safety promising their service to God? Once out of danger, what then? How many mothers plead to God for their children in crisis promising more devotion to God? Once a mother's child is distanced from that crisis, is God the mother's first devotion or is the child who she loves with all her heart? People make deals all the time with God when they are in trouble then we forget Him. Our loyalty to God dissolves until the next crisis.

Can you begin to appreciate God's patience and mercy with men?

Again the Israelites did evil in the eyes of the LORD. They served the Baals and the Ashtoreths, and the gods of Aram, the gods of Sidon, the gods of Moab, the gods of the Ammonites and the gods of the Philistines.

Judges 10:6 (NIV)

Again the Israelites did evil in the eyes of the LORD, so the LORD delivered them into the hands of the Philistines for forty years.

Judges 13:1 (NIV)

(Samson delivered Israel that time)

Only God could save them from their oppressors that sometimes He had sent. Throughout the Old Testament we see a faithful God dealing with a fickle people. Today we must admit we are no better. Maybe, if people are all the same, we will not call out to God until the agony of oppression is so unbearable that we, as a people, cry out to God with repentant hearts.

Just after the terrible events of 9-11, America had a moment of acknowledging God. The ACLU and AUSCS (Americans United for Separation of Church and State) were silent as politicians from both sides of the fence sang together for God's blessing and prayed out loud asking for God's protection and guidance. Why? Because nobody was going to tell us in such a horrible crisis that we couldn't cry out to God. Then, like the Israelites, once things felt more comfortable it was OK again to tell people not to pray in public, not to display manger scenes on public property, not to pray at graduations, etc.

Over and over again the sons of Israel did evil in the sight of the Lord, and repeatedly God Himself would give them over to plunderers or oppressors. Every time the sons of Israel were in serious enough bondage they would then cry out to God and He would once again deliver them. Read this for yourself in the book of Judges in your own Bible.

The church isn't experiencing righteous persecution, friends. This is God's judgment. We should be grateful for his faithful correction and repent.

Must we, in America, go into even greater bondage before we repent and cry out to the Lord?

Tomorrow never comes. We cannot repent tomorrow. Today is the only time we can do anything. Our work for righteousness must begin today.

You may have heard the definition for insanity as doing the same thing over and over while hoping for a different result.

APATHY IS NOT THE PEACE THAT PASSES UNDERSTANDING

> Woe to you who are complacent in Zion, and to you who feel secure on Mount Samaria, you notable men of the foremost nation, to whom the people of Israel come! Therefore you will be among the first to go into exile; your feasting and lounging will end.
>
> **Amos 6:1, 7 (NIV)**

God's judgment is not upon us just because millions of babies are murdered by killers certified as doctors and hired by the babies' own mothers. No, it is because God's people hardly lift a finger to save these innocents. How can this happen, legal now for more than 40 years, in "one nation under God"? How can we do this and say "God Bless America"?

If a man assaults a pregnant woman and kills the baby it is murder. If the mother wants the baby dead it is her "controlling her body". Depending who wants the baby dead determines whether it is murder or a legal right.

AIDS, venereal disease, legal greed, and many horrors don't upset God as much as His own people not being disturbed enough to challenge society's flagrant opposition to what is right.

Do you see all the TV shows showing what the Bible calls "fornication", "adultery", and "homosexuality" as good material for humorous, popular entertainment topics? Not sometimes but every day, all day.

The Author of Life, the Lord of lords, Creator of all that exists, is lowered by scientific magazines, educational TV programs, museums, and every public classroom from elementary school to graduate school to some silly old religious fable since "there is no creator".

The teachings of Christ are outlawed while Indian tales, Halloween stories, witchcraft, and eastern religions are treated with utmost respect. It is considered ignorant to mock various religions yet somewhat hip to mock Christ, Christianity, and the Lord God.

Maybe the reason so many Americans consistently get into God's face with contempt for Him is because God so clearly condemns many of the things that are everyday life to us. They resent feeling disapproved of by God.

So what do we do? Who do we serve?

Although it may be comforting to sit in a room filled with 10,000 or 100,000 believers that applaud God, wickedness is not threatened until our convictions enter *the arena of life* . . . family, work, school, community, law, government, organizations, and church too.

Church is the launch-pad and refuge for healing. It is NOT our private island. It is NOT a launch-pad for business contacts or a safe place to quote scripture and discuss the world's sins.

My warning taken from Amos 6:1,7 is this: "Woe to us who are at ease in the church, and to us who feel secure yet have not grieved over the ruin of America enough to do anything except complain—therefore we have now gone into exile."

It is God Who chooses for us to live intelligently (true wisdom) but WE decide whether we will conform to His will or not.

It is God Who teaches righteousness but it is WE who must practice it.

It is God Who calls us to repentance but it is WE who must repent.

We cannot continue as we have and hope for revival and change. It is crazy to expect good fruit from disobedience.

CHAPTER FIVE

✦ ✦ ✦

Attitudes Toward Justice

THE BIBLICAL ATTITUDE TOWARD LAW ENFORCEMENT

Imagine all government positions filled with Christians. Would it be right for Christians to abolish law enforcement and punishment of criminals in order to be forgiving to everyone? This would be scripturally wrong and a huge crime to society.

This certainly would not be the righteousness that would exalt a nation. This would reap anarchy. Criminals and bullies of every kind would dominate every community.

There is biblical advice to people who are in a position of administering judgment:

> He who says to the wicked, "You are righteous and innocent", peoples will curse him, nations will defy and abhor him. But to those [upright judges] who rebuke the wicked it is well and they will find delight and a good blessing will be upon them.
>
> **Proverbs 24:24-25 (AMP)**

It is appropriate to equate uprightness with Christianity but we have heard little about rebuking the wicked. To do otherwise will leave us cursed at, defied and abhorred, as explained by wise Solomon in the above verse.

The Bible is explicit,

> ...law is not made for a righteous man, but for those who are lawless and rebellious, for the ungodly and sinners, for the unholy and profane, for those who kill their fathers or mothers, for murderers and immoral men and homosexuals and kidnappers and liars and perjurers, and whatever else is contrary to sound teaching...
>
> **1 Timothy 1:9-10 (NASB)**

The law is a guide. Within its boundaries is a guide for the realm of conscience. The Bible is an especially wise guide. But the law communicates to all its citizens what society threatens to those that choose to cross those boundaries the law has drawn.

"If you cross this line we will have to protect others and ourselves from you".

It is more than a threat. It is a guide to those not wanting to cross that line. This is also like safety and health laws providing minimum standards for the public. It can be educational as well as threatening because to the citizen it is declaring right and wrong.

Another fair comparison would be the guardrail on the edge of a highway overlooking homes. The guardrail is there for the protection of the driver and also the homes below. Good drivers may never notice the guardrail is there. Poor drivers may complain how they keep scratching and denting their cars on those deterrents (the guardrails).

There are always those whining about how laws suppress and restrict their creativity or freedom of expression.

If you think about it, the arguments go a little like this:

"Who are we to restrict driving styles?"

"Why should cars suffer injury from guard rails?"

"Hey, it's their car anyway."

"No one has the right to dictate how they should drive."

We are the cars. The guard rails are laws. Driving styles are lifestyles. In reality, we all affect one another. That is simply inescapable. Freedom can be granted but only to the point where it begins invading others' freedom. The law is very much a "parent" that dictates to us right and wrong. A sheriff or policeman enforces our laws. It is not the policeman's duty to persuade an offender that the law is good; only to enforce that law.

None of us would want someone to exercise their freedom of expression selling poisonous tuna fish. We know the poison is harmful. Although there may be controversy about exactly where to draw the line on what is indecent, we already know statistically that pornography is a main diet for 100% of every sex offender in America. If a drug killed one or more people, the FDA (Food and Drug Administration) would investigate and likely declare the drug unsafe and pull it off the market. Pornography has been the inspiration of many crimes, including murder and rape but this product gets to call itself "freedom of expression" irregardless of the harm it does. Billions of dollars can buy plenty of lobbying I guess.

Still others may argue the law is too restrictive, "*Take down the guardrails, people will crash through those guard rails anyway. People have always crashed through guardrails. We can't change human nature.*"

Once we take down the guardrails and laws, we are telling citizens, "It is now OK to drive off the cliff injuring yourself and others below." Should we legalize drunk driving because people have always enjoyed intoxication for thousands of years? Should we legalize drunk driving because people will always drink no matter what laws we pass? Easing laws is not only removing restrictions; it adds an endorsement to what was once illegal. It tells those who have no personal convictions and the young that there is no legal reason to restrict them from this now lawful activity.

GOOD AND BAD LAWS

It is not the government that writes laws. It is the people through the government that writes laws.

Since all of society is usually more likely to perceive many of its values and a public sense of right and wrong from its laws, it is important for Christians to be pro-active in the making of those laws.

Now look at laws that protect the guilty, that protect the right to kill unborn babies and laws that call pornography "freedom of expression". These are not laws misused but examples of using the power of legislation to make flat out bad laws.

I often hear people complain about groups of people "taking our money". Whether welfare recipients, illegal immigrants, or foreign nations; none of these are taking anyone's money. Government officials are *giving away* that money, rightfully in some cases and wrongfully in others. The point is, don't get upset at people who are willing to take money given to them. They do not have the power to twist the government's arm for free money. If you disagree with whom money is given to don't get upset with the recipient. Through taxes you hand money over to the government, and then they do what they want with it.

The Bible teaches us to obey the law. Paul teaches to obey the law. The Bible teaches us to be on the side of the law. We cannot shrug off bad laws by disobeying laws. Laws are good. I will quote scriptures on this in just a few pages. The Bible says laws are good and when you think it through, it is true. We all need to recognize the simple truth of that. When we see it, the importance of our involvement in lawmaking becomes easier to see. Civilized societies absolutely need law and enforcement of the law.

ENFORCEMENT OF LAW

It is vital to understand that merely putting a law on the books is not a sufficient deterrent. It must be enforced. Un-enforced law is not law, but merely a suggestion. If the law is un-enforced, it may be worse than no law. It mocks the whole concept of law. Many assume that once a law is on the books the matter is taken care of. This is why we so need Christian attorneys, judges, juries, police and detectives who know their duty and will do it – honorably, diligently, consistently.

> The execution of justice is joy for the righteous,
> But it is terror to the workers of iniquity.
>
> **Proverbs 21:15 (NASB)**

Believers rejoice when good laws are enforced; not because they want vengeance, but because the innocent and weak are protected from crime. Additionally, those contemplating certain wrong actions may well be discouraged after they see the consequences of breaking the law.

God is the original lawmaker and He Himself imposes both blessing and calamity. Just as there are His physical laws *of* action, there are His moral laws *for* action. The consequences of breaking these laws are equally consistent both in the physical and spiritual realm. His laws for proper conduct are a guide and so it is with the laws of the land.

Christians must see that proper laws are passed, and they must also see that these laws are upheld promptly, consistently and impartially.

OUR CURRENT WRONG ATTITUDE

Our attitude and action in regard to law is stated simply in Micah:

> He hath showed thee, O man, what is good; and what doth the Lord require of thee, but to do justly, and to love mercy, and to walk humbly with thy God.
>
> **Micah 6:8 (KJV)**

Not only can good laws be wrongfully used but there can also be improper attitudes toward justice and law enforcement in our present society. Have you noticed how the crowds cheer as the bad guy gets his head blasted off at the movie theater? This thirst for vengeful justice is a constant theme in TV shows and movies. This yearning, lusting for justice is a natural backlash to our "civilized" tolerance to nearly every kind of lifestyle.

This mentality is also contrary to a God who demands "Vengeance is mine".

Back In the 1960's and 1970's, our courts and too many of our psychological circles seemed almost ridiculous in their excusing of the criminal mind. Although seemingly compassionate to the offender, it invited more crime by its "winking" at repeat offenders.

Now I see the pendulum swinging the other way in the public attitude. There has been a rightful growing anger toward repeat offenders and child molesters. The popularity of the bad guys getting what they deserve has gone from the movie screens in the 70's to a plethora of cop shows on TV today. "Get the bad guys" is what the public obviously wants. It is the logical reaction to the lack of justice in our courts every day. Neither the mercy of the court or the vengeance of the public is the biblical attitude God requires in Micah 6:8 (above).

The protection of society (the community) has always been important to God throughout the scripture.

Of course, there is tremendous pressure for being politically correct from the philosophy of "live and let live". This is often construed as the flag of "love". It is subtle deception. It is contrary to truth and scripture. In conformity to this dictate, many fear pointing their finger and stating disapproval of any lifestyle. Instead of the courtroom, the movie-makers give us the justice we crave. But it is fiction. We fear man more than God.

We continue to inwardly yearn for justice and our hearts become bitter and void of real love. Few see how this is exactly the opposite of what God wants from us, which is to DO justice BUT love mercy. This is doing right while craving mercy for others.

THE RIGHT ATTITUDE

Now can you understand how our attitude permeates our nation today? Instead of "doing mercy" while secretly or openly yearning for justice, God wants us to DO JUSTICE with an inward yearning to grant mercy.

The true Christ-like person is unrelenting in regard to the law. Whether the criminal is rich, poor, old, young, friend, family, or foe;

the Christian looks for an opportunity to show mercy but without ever compromising the justice owed to society and the victims.

Here it is again:

> He has showed you, O man, what is good. And what does the Lord require of you? To act justly and to love mercy and to walk humbly with your God.
>
> **Micah 6:8 (NIV)**

This is the biblical attitude toward law and its enforcement. This attitude should prompt many Christians to get involved in establishing righteousness in every arena.

We do not attack those we hate. If we hate at all, we have completely and unquestionably abandoned all that God has required of us. Once we give in to the carnal passion of merciless justice, we become willing enemies of God Himself. As far as faking mercy while rendering justice—good luck trying to con God. That's called hypocrisy and as far as I can remember, religious hypocrites were the only folks Jesus showed literal anger toward.

LAW—A MINISTER OF GOD

Scripture advocates obeying the laws of the land.

> Those who forsake the law praise the wicked, but those who keep the law strive with them.
>
> **Proverbs 28:4 (NASB)**

The old adage, "You can't fight City Hall" is not found in scripture nor is anything like that encouraged in the Bible. Believers and unbelievers can and do win against unjust rulings and laws.

But what about laws that are contrary to God's principles? It is not a matter of civil disobedience in America. It is a matter of getting laws changed to correspond with the laws of God. We are the "establishment" and if we are not, that is what we need to aspire to. It is a much greater victory for righteousness to create good laws or to replace bad laws with good laws. Certainly it requires more patience and strength, but it ministers to many more people.

To get away with breaking a bad law serves no one but ourselves and begins to erode respect for the law in general. It is not our calling.

Rome was obviously not a Christian nation, yet Paul commanded the Christians in Rome:

> Let every person be in subjection to the governing authorities. For there is no authority except from God and those which exist are established by God. Therefore he who resists authority has opposed the ordinance of God; and they who have opposed will receive condemnation upon themselves. For rulers are not a cause of fear for good behavior, but for evil. Do you want to have no fear of authority? Do what is good, and you will have praise from the same; for it is a minister of God to you for good. But if you do what is evil, be afraid; for it does not bear the sword for nothing; for it is a minister of God, an avenger who brings wrath upon the one who practices evil. Wherefore it is necessary to be in subjection, not only because of wrath, but also for conscience' sake. For because of this you also pay taxes, for [rulers] are servants of God, devoting themselves to this very thing.
>
> **Romans 13:1-6 (NASB)**

Behold, Paul declares Roman law, laid down by pagans as a "minister of God". Twice he calls this secular law "a minister of God". Nowhere does Paul urge civil disobedience. Remember, Rome had invaded and conquered the Jews and ruled over them against their will.

We cannot say Paul didn't understand that we are citizens of a corrupt government. Rome was dominating the Jewish nation at the time Paul wrote this.

Paul even calls the rulers "servants of God" in the above passage.

Listen, if secular, political, and legal rulers are *servants of God* and law is the *minister of God*, why should any Christian ever consider political leadership an "ungodly" or "unscriptural" pursuit? How dare any Christian consider political or legal leadership to be below the call of God!

The righteous obviously should pursue such leadership positions even as a godly career. All types of leadership positions, whether judges, legislators, or governors should be filled with servants of God. More than anyone else, more than the corrupt, more than the ambitious, more than the rich, more than the hundreds of causes out there, followers of Jesus should desire to be legal and governmental leaders. One should aspire to be the "minister of God" and the "servant of God" that Paul refers to, thus ministering faithfulness to the Lord and His principles to the people. What an honor.

Politics is an honorable profession; more so for any person who does it as a service to God and the community.

Politics and politicians have a bad reputation as liars and promise-breakers. Many are just that. Politics involves constantly being criticized publicly by those who disagree with the politician. It is not an easy job, yet these same men and women make laws and policy and influence appointments of people to important posts. They also direct much of the tax dollar to what they want. It is after getting in office that they learn all the back office agendas, compromising, and favors-for-favors. They ARE the government as elected officials. God's people need to be here. Shall we merely conclude the enemies of God have more backbone than those who love God? Shall we excuse ourselves by saying corruption is prophesied for the last days? Shall we simply admit that others are willing to get dirty, be accused and get into the fight to help others but we are not? May it never be.

CHAPTER SIX

✦ ✦ ✦

God Still Requires Holiness

MERCY IS NOT UNHOLINESS

True religion releases us from bondage. It separates us from sin. It brings us to the banqueting table of His great love and mercy. His grace is our feast and we serve Him because His goodness leads us to continual repentance.

> ...and said to Jesus,
> "Teacher, this woman was caught in the act of adultery. In the Law Moses commanded us to stone such women. Now what do you say?" They were using this question as a trap, in order to have a basis for accusing him. But Jesus bent down and started to write on the ground with his finger. When they kept on questioning him, he straightened up and said to them, "If any one of you is without sin, let him be the first to throw a stone at her." Again he stooped down and wrote on the ground. At this, those who heard began to go away one at a time, the older ones first, until only Jesus was left, with the woman still standing there. Jesus straightened up and asked her, "Woman, where are they? Has no one condemned you?" "No one, sir," she said. "Then neither do I condemn you," Jesus declared.

> "Go now and leave your life of sin."
>
> **John 8:4-11 (NIV)**

"Then neither do I condemn you" Jesus said. But I thought that God condemned adultery? Did not God ordain the stoning for adultery? Doesn't God want to protect families from adultery? The answers are "yes", "yes", and "yes".

> ...Jesus said "He who has seen Me has seen the Father...
>
> **John 14:9 (NASB)**

Jesus is the very representation of God's true character. Does God hate adulterers? No. God has never hated adulterers for one second. However, He does hate adultery specifically because of what it does to everyone, including the adulterers He so dearly loves. This is true of murderers, thieves, homosexuals, liars, and religious hypocrites too. I am truly not trying to be offensive but simply echoing scripture. To the list it adds: drunkards, fornicators, and even those who covet. I am not the name-caller, the Bible is. God knows every human heart, which is why He is so very specific regarding dangers.

> Do you not know that the wicked will not inherit the kingdom of God? Do not be deceived: Neither the sexually immoral nor idolaters nor adulterers nor male prostitutes nor homosexual offenders nor thieves nor the greedy nor drunkards nor slanderers nor swindlers will inherit the kingdom of God.
>
> **1 Corinthians 6:9-10 (NIV)**

These lifestyles are not foreign to the church. This is what the church is made up of in the book of Corinthians, but they repented of those things. See the very next verse:

> And such were some of you: but ye are washed, but ye are sanctified, but ye are justified in the name of the Lord Jesus, and by the Spirit of our God.
>
> **1 Corinthians 6:11 (KJV)**

They are all sinful ways of living, which according to God isn't a good thing. God always loves the sinner and always hates the sin. He hates sin because He loves people. Even coveting is wrong. You can be poor but always coveting or craving what the rich have. "Why can't I have that?" You are in trouble with God. He sees you ignoring the good things in your life that He is giving you but more importantly, you are making yourself unhappy and God wants you to be happy. That is the main reason God wants to take away our sin, because He wants to make room for better choices, better consequences, better relationships, better wisdom, a better you, and happiness.

The adulteress knew her sin. The crowd about to stone her hadn't owned up to their own sins. Then Jesus said:

> If any one of you is without sin, let him be the first to throw a stone at her.
>
> **John 8:7b (NIV)**

THE NEW TESTAMENT STILL REQUIRES HOLINESS

People have often considered what Jesus did with the adulteress as an ushering in of "No more judging". As though anyone who has ever sinned has no right to ever condemn sin. That idea is almost a final blow to holiness. But notice Jesus NEVER said adultery was not a sin. He said that He did not condemn her, but He gave her an important command,

> Go now and leave your life of sin.
>
> **John 8:11 (NIV)**

Many have expressed relief that they did not live in the old, strict days of the law. They do not understand that Jesus never lowered the standards in the New Testament. In truth, Jesus made the standards higher. Here again is Jesus talking.

> You have heard that it was said, "Do not commit adultery."
> But I tell you that anyone who looks at a woman lustfully
> has already committed adultery with her in his heart.
>
> **Matthew 5:27-28 (NIV)**

Where did anyone get the idea that holiness has been replaced by faith? It is ONLY by faith in Jesus Christ that we are saved, and Jesus Christ clearly reveals that holiness and obedience are still issues.

After Jesus' resurrection, remember the couple that thought it OK to lie? They were even donating money to the church and they simply lied about the donation.

> But a certain man named Ananias, with his wife Sapphira, sold a piece of property, and kept back [some] of the price for himself, with his wife's full knowledge, and bringing a portion of it, he laid it at the apostles' feet. But Peter said, "Ananias, why has Satan filled your heart to lie to the Holy Spirit, and to keep back [some] of the price of the land? While it remained [unsold], did it not remain your own? And after it was sold, was it not under your control? Why is it that you have conceived this deed in your heart? You have not lied to men, but to God. "And as he heard these words, Ananias fell down and breathed his last; and great fear came upon all who heard of it. And the young men arose and covered him up, and after carrying him out, they buried him. Now there elapsed an interval of about three hours, and his wife came in, not knowing what had happened. And Peter responded to her, "Tell me whether you sold the land for such and such a price?" And she said, "Yes, that was the price. "Then Peter [said] to her, "Why is it that you have agreed together to put the Spirit of the Lord to the test? Behold, the feet of those who have buried your husband are at the door, and they shall carry you out [as well]"And she fell immediately at his feet, and breathed her last; and the young men came in and found her dead, and they carried her out and buried her beside her husband.
>
> **Acts 5:1-10 (NASB)**

Whoops! Holiness is still important in the New Testament? Jesus died for Ananias and Sapphira, so their sins could be forgiven. God is merciful, but mercy is and was never intended to be a compromise of holiness. Holiness IS still required of His people.

This next scripture shows an *unbeliever* being killed by one of God's angels for robbing God of His glory.

> And on an appointed day Herod, having put on his royal apparel, took his seat on the rostrum and [began] delivering an address to them. And the people kept crying out, "The voice of a god and not of a man!" And immediately an angel of the Lord struck him because he did not give God the glory, and he was eaten by worms and died.
>
> **Acts 12:21-23 (NASB)**

My friends, we must join the Holy Spirit and stop resisting Him in His quest to prepare the Bride of Christ, to usher in the second coming of Christ. He wants us to please our Father and the Father wants us to be free of sin so we can experience more and more joy and more and more freedom. He wants us to reconcile as many as possible to Christ because it is not God's Will that any should perish, but that all come *to repentance*—"TO REPENTANCE"

> The Lord is not slow about His promise,
> as some count slowness, but is patient toward you,
> not wishing for any to perish but for all to come to repentance.
>
> **2 Peter 3:9 (NASB)**

The mercy of God has never been about excusing sin but rather saving *from* sin. We must speak the truth about these matters because we love God and we love the people that live with us in this generation. Surely, we must love those that would be His Church, Christ's Bride, Zion, the sons of God. It certainly IS NOT God's Will that some perish. Read the scripture again. He desires ALL to come to repentance.

Isaiah, in his zeal for God and God's vision, refused to be silent. God's vision is for doing right. We benefit when we do right. We are ruined by bad choices piled on bad choices and saved by turning from incorrect choices to wise choices piled on more good choices.

For Zion's sake I will not keep silent,
for Jerusalem's sake I will not remain quiet,
till her righteousness shines out like the dawn,
her salvation like a blazing torch.

Isaiah 62:1 (NIV)

HOLINESS THAT HIDES ISN'T HOLY

You can hide from involvement, but not from God. God commands involvement. Observe the following scriptures. God is pointing His finger at those in Zion who are not doing anything for anybody except themselves.

Woe to you who are complacent in Zion,
and to you who feel secure on Mount Samaria,
you notable men of the foremost nation,
to whom the people of Israel come!

Amos 6:1 (NIV)

When God says, "Woe to you", that is being cursed by God. Needless to say, that is real serious trouble when you are cursed by God.

All of Israel is in trouble and they will go into exile. A few verses later He condemns one tribe for not grieving over the afflictions of His people in another tribe of Israel, the tribe of Joseph.

That would be like, horrible laws being passed in New York that are terribly oppressive to the righteous, and the Christians in California shrugging their shoulders and saying, "So what? New York is like that. Thank God that didn't happen here" and then going on in their comforts.

God gets mad and promises them to be first in line for exile.

You drink wine by the bowlful and use the finest lotions,
but you do not grieve over the ruin of Joseph.

> Therefore you will be among the first to go into exile;
> your feasting and lounging will end.
>
> **Amos 6:6-7 (NIV)**

I hope as you are reading you are noticing that these judgments are not on the world or the unbelievers. All of these scriptures apply to God's people. God's prophets are speaking God's condemnation on God's people for not repenting of their sins. When sin abounds among God's people, the world has no light to guide them. How can we lead a nation if we are misleading our own families?

> For it is time for judgment to begin with the household of God; and if [it begins] with us first, what will be the outcome for those who do not obey the gospel of God?
>
> **1 Peter 4:17 (NASB)**

HOLINESS WITHOUT LOVE ISN'T HOLY

There is something universally agreed upon among most people in the world for thousands of years; the worthlessness of a person with no vices or bad habits who is religious but when it comes to other people, they are cold-hearted. God is not calling us to be "better" but rather, loving. This is the point; we are scripturally ignorant if we think for one second that we can be righteous or holy without loving others. When will the church agree with God, Jesus, and the scriptures on this point? To not love IS sin.

Take love out of holiness and it has nothing to do with God's holiness. When we truly love, we see the stupidity of sin and we WANT to repent. When we truly love we DON'T WANT to get away with sin, we want to get away *from* sin. When loving people condemn sin it is entirely different from self-righteous hypocrites condemning people they want to look down upon.

It is not enough to just read and nod in approval. Read this and understand the warning:

> If the people of the community close their eyes when that man gives one of his children to Molech and they fail to put him to death, I will set my face against that man and his family and will cut off from their people both him and all who follow him in prostituting themselves to Molech.
>
> **Leviticus 20:4-5 (NIV)**

God has promised to set His face against the man and his family who refuse to lift a finger against the sin in his own community! Apparently as far as God is concerned, silence is consent.

This scripture portion is a call to confront.

Do WE know what is right and what is wrong? Do we keep it to ourselves or do we share what we have and know?

Do we just talk to those that agree with us or do we enter the arena to burst light into the darkness?

Scriptural principle says that if we have more, God requires more from us.

> But the one who does not know and does things deserving punishment will be beaten with few blows. From everyone who has been given much, much will be demanded; and from the one who has been entrusted with much, much more will be asked.
>
> **Luke 12:48 (NIV)**

When phony Christians talk about love or the hypocrite about righteousness, it falls flat for everyone except for other phonies and hypocrites. One of the best ways to neutralize the impact of truth is to have whackos and fakes spotlighted as the messengers. I see that portrayed all the time on TV and in movies. Where are the respectable, sincere and truly loving Christians that are spreading the true gospel?

> Like a lame man's legs that hang limp is a proverb
> in the mouth of a fool.
>
> **Proverbs 26:7 (NIV)**

CHURCH MEMBERSHIP ISN'T HOLINESS

To a needy world and those who are completely willing to obey all that Jesus asks, the phonies and the fakes are obvious, embarrassingly obvious. There is a huge difference between those who are serving the needy and those who are exploiting the needy for their own glory or gain.

Still, multitudes are easily deceived. Scams are for profit, whether it be a diet pill or a religion. So many teachers and denominations are promising heaven just for being members of the "true faith"—such a deal, huh? "Just sign here and you are saved." "Just worship with us and you get to live forever." "Just give us 10% and you'll surely go to heaven." "But if you dare to leave our denomination, you will surely go to hell." "Even sin is tolerable as long as you stay with us, the one true faith." "No matter how loving, holy, and obedient you are—if you are not in our denomination, you will never be acceptable to God."

I can barely believe the large number of religious men who arrogantly impersonate God. They pretend to determine everyone's eternity based on membership. Think about it. There are so many denominations claiming those outside their denomination are destined for hell unless they become a member of their denomination.

Imagine Judgment Day and saying, "But my church said I would live forever like everyone else at our church."

Yeah, but what does your Bible say? It isn't your membership, but your life.

I have cringed hearing overconfident public statements condemning those that believe differently than the "True Church". There are hundreds of different denominations and many claim that they alone are the "True Church".

Such religious leaders are those that persecute God's faithful and consider themselves doing a service for God.

> They will make you outcasts from the synagogue,
> but an hour is coming for everyone who kills you
> to think that he is offering service to God.
>
> **John 16:2 (NASB)**

Dear reader, there is only one true church. It is not a denomination. Jesus loves people, not organizations. Jesus died to save people, all people; not institutions. Therefore, God knows those who respond to Him. God knows precisely who is responding to Him and who is resisting Him. The Bible clarifies this point. Paul put it this way:

> Nevertheless, the firm foundation of God stands, having this seal, "The Lord knows those who are His," and, "Let everyone who names the name of the Lord abstain from wickedness."
>
> **2 Timothy 2:19 (NASB)**

Be careful that you are part of His Church—not man's religious membership. There is no Bible verse guaranteeing salvation for the right membership anymore than the right ethnic group or nation. Join Him by obeying Him and loving all.

Holiness is part of God's call to every one of His people. Yes, every one of us are sinners saved by grace, however, that is not to say that every one of us have been *excused* by grace. No. Grace is not a license to sin; it is a license for holiness. We are being saved FROM sin. Hallelujah! In place of ignorance and error, God is putting wisdom and love.

Please remember that everything is contagious, both sin and righteousness; cowardice and courage; complaint and thankfulness; prejudice and love; running away from the battle line or running to it.

If we will be uncompromising – it WILL affect others.

There is a difference when obedient servants of God are leaders instead of diligently corrupt personalities.

> When the righteous thrive, the people rejoice;
> when the wicked rule, the people groan.
>
> **Proverbs 29:2 (NIV)**

CHAPTER SEVEN

✦ ✦ ✦

The Largest Cult in the World

There is no benefit to believing a lie, but this is the big deception: Knowing the truth is *not* living the truth. The truth ignored, is not enlightenment but greater condemnation according to the Bible. Greater condemnation comes when we know what is right but refuse to yield to it.

> Therefore, to one who knows the right thing to do, and does not do it, to him it is sin.
>
> **James 4:17 (NASB)**

A cult is by definition, a sect contrary to the truth. Naturally, what is the true religion to one group is a cult to another. Consider the ridiculousness of this mentality as it is more simply stated: "Hypocrisy has no consequences for those who believe like me." "Whoever believes like me is going to heaven." "Whoever is a member of my religion is righteous." "The more you know the more favor you have with God."

Consider again the prior scripture. It is not knowing the truth, but rather doing it, that gains benefit. What I am explaining to you is well understood by people in every culture on the planet. It is understood by people within every religion. It is taught in almost every religion and simply stated it is this: Humble people that truly care about others are more righteous than angry religious types who hate. Doctrine is NOT more important than lifestyle.

I hope, dear reader, you understand without reservation that neither doctrine nor membership is the proof of anyone's character.

It is sheer manipulation of the masses when religious leaders convince a person that agreeing with them is more important than living humbly in service to your fellow man. I will back up these statements with scripture soon. It is simply a crazy idea that doctrine is more important than lifestyle.

True religion never gives license for sin. Our repentance to serving Christ gives us inspiration to live a life of love and honesty, with hope and joy that it is reasonable and has value, now and eternally. This is our faith. God is watching and rewarding all; both evil and good. What we are now, germinates into our eternal destiny. This is true for our loved ones as well.

But be ye doers of the word, and not hearers only, deceiving your own selves.

James 1:22 (KJV)

If ye know these things, happy are ye if ye do them.

John 13:17 (KJV)

Even without the Bible, folks have a general sense for what is true. Nobody trusts a liar. Nobody likes to see someone say they believe one thing and then turn around and do the opposite. We all know instinctively that a right life is far more righteous than a right belief.

Of course, the right belief is very crucial.

and you shall know the truth, and the truth shall make you free.

John 8:32 (NASB)

The point is that KNOWING is not as important as DOING. The reason God gives us truth is entirely so we can stop DOING wrong, start DOING right, and reap the benefits of a better life.

It is faith that spurs one to commit more virtuous deeds and although it is impossible to please God without faith, it is by our deeds that we are judged. Read the following scriptures. I have capitalized some words for focus:

> ...those who did the GOOD DEEDS to a resurrection of life, those who committed the EVIL DEEDS to a resurrection of judgment.
>
> **John 5:29 (NASB)**

> For the Son of Man is going to come in the glory of His Father with His angels; And WILL THEN RECOMPENSE [REPAY] EVERY MAN ACCORDING TO HIS DEEDS.
>
> **Matthew 16:27 (NASB)**

> who WILL RENDER TO EVERY MAN ACCORDING TO HIS DEEDS: to those who by PERSEVERANCE IN DOING GOOD seek for glory and honor and immortality, eternal life; but to those who are selfishly ambitious and do not obey the truth, but obey unrighteousness, wrath and indignation.
>
> **Romans 2:6-8 (NASB)**

> They profess to know God, but BY THEIR DEEDS they deny Him, being detestable and disobedient, and worthless for any good deed.
>
> **Titus 1:16 (NASB)**

> ...and all the churches will know that I am He who searches the minds and hearts; and I will give to each one of you ACCORDING TO YOUR DEEDS
>
> **Revelation 2:23 (NASB)**

> ...and the dead were judged from the things which were written in the books, ACCORDING TO THEIR DEEDS.
>
> **Revelation 20:12 (NASB)**

...and they were judged, every one of them ACCORDING TO THEIR DEEDS.

Revelation 20:13 (NASB)

For we must all appear before the judgment seat of Christ, that each one may be RECOMPENSED FOR HIS DEEDS IN THE BODY, ACCORDING TO WHAT HE HAS DONE, whether good or bad.

2 Corinthians 5:10 (NASB)

And if you address as Father the One who IMPARTIALLY JUDGES ACCORDING TO EACH MAN'S WORK, conduct yourselves in fear during the time of your stay upon earth;

1 Peter 1:17 (NASB)

I, the LORD, search the heart, I test the mind, Even to give to each man ACCORDING TO HIS WAYS, According to the RESULTS OF HIS DEEDS.

Jeremiah 17:10 (NASB)

It is not for religious virtue that I condemn hypocrisy in myself. It is because I find no use for stupidity in missing God's blessings that I condemn all hypocrisy in myself. I want the benefits of obeying God. Who am I fooling if I convince everyone that I'm a good person but incur God's anger?

The Bible teaches love, honesty, kindness, forgiveness, mercy, compassion on the poor, justice, and repentance when wrong [which means if you are doing the wrong thing, stop doing it and start doing the right thing]. These characteristics are universally respected. Every enduring hero has exhibited one or more of these qualities whether in life, history, or even in fiction.

What we all know in our heart and what is also universally recognized is that a kind, loving, just man who may be ignorant in the ways of religious doctrine deserves more respect than someone who believes right but is unkind, unloving and dishonest.

Every single religion has in its ranks those who are haughty and arrogant assuming their knowledge puts them above others. Every single religion also has in its ranks that person of quality who is kind-hearted and generous with the needy. That quality of human that grieves when anyone suffers and rejoices when others achieve earned success and sometimes unearned mercy is always admirable.

Even Jesus didn't like it when folks criticized others while they had so many of their own flaws, which are sometimes worse.

> And why do you look at the speck that is in your brother's eye, but do not notice the log that is in your own eye? Or how can you say to your brother, "Let me take the speck out of your eye," and behold, the log is in your own eye? You hypocrite, first take the log out of your own eye, and then you will see clearly to take the speck out of your brother's eye.
>
> **Matthew 7:3-5 (NASB)**

Our most important words are not words. People aren't as stupid as many assume. They watch our lives and if you volunteer words they will also look to see how well your walk lines up with your talk.

> You are our letter, written in our hearts, known and read by all men; being manifested that you are a letter of Christ, cared for by us, written not with ink, but with the Spirit of the living God, not on tablets of stone, but on tablets of human hearts.
>
> **2 Corinthians 3:2-3 (NASB)**

Here it is again in a different translation.

> You yourselves are our letter, written on our hearts, known and read by everybody. You show that you are a letter from Christ, the result of our ministry, written not with ink but with the Spirit of the living God, not on tablets of stone but on tablets of human hearts.
>
> **2 Corinthians 3:2-3 (NIV)**

DENOMINATIONALISM

We *all* need a slight dose of disrespect for our own denomination in deference to Jesus Christ and the Word of God. Any denomination that demands loyalty to itself above Jesus and the Bible proves Christ and the Word of God is NOT its supreme authority. Be careful; heed the advice from the New American Standard, New International Version, and the King James Version:

> But do not be called Rabbi; for One is your Teacher, and you are all brothers. And do not call [anyone] on earth your father; for One is your Father, He who is in heaven. And do not be called leaders; for One is your Leader, [that is,] Christ. But the greatest among you shall be your servant.
>
> **Matthew 23:8-11 (NASB)**

> But you are not to be called 'Rabbi,' for you have only one Master and you are all brothers. And do not call anyone on earth 'father,' for you have one Father, and he is in heaven. Nor are you to be called 'teacher,' for you have one Teacher, the Christ. The greatest among you will be your servant.
>
> **Matthew 23:8-11 (NIV)**

> But be not ye called Rabbi: for one is your Master, [even] Christ; and all ye are brethren. And call no [man] your father upon the earth: for one is your Father, which is in heaven. Neither be ye called masters: for one is your Master, [even] Christ.But he that is greatest among you shall be your servant.
>
> **Matthew 23:8-11 (KJV)**

Remember, *everything is contagious*: attitudes, courage, cowardice, obedience, compromise, repentance, stubbornness, love, hate, zeal, boredom; no matter what you do—it will reproduce around you.

The real stuff that the Lord wants in us always begins privately between you and Jesus.

In all your ways acknowledge Him, and He will make your paths straight.

Proverbs 3:6 (NASB)

CHAPTER EIGHT

✦ ✦ ✦

See Past The Words

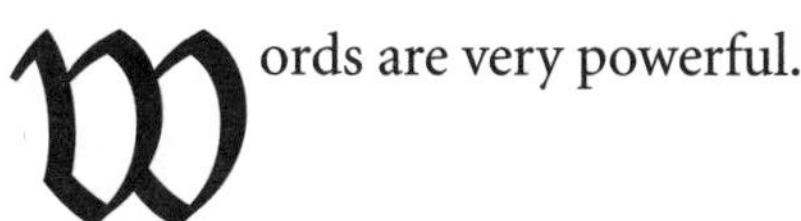

ords are very powerful.

Death and life are in the power of the tongue, and those who love it will eat its fruit.

Proverbs 18:21 (NASB)

The tongue has the power of life and death, and those who love it will eat its fruit.

Proverbs 18:21 (NIV)

MAKE BELIEVE HUMILITY

Judge not, that ye be not judged.

Matthew 7:1 (KJV)

This is a very frequently quoted scripture that is intended to keep us humble and compassionate but has become an excuse for doing nothing.

There is a lie out of the heart of hell which many believers embrace. The wording gives the appearance of humility but it is a deceptive concept that is contrary to scripture. You may have heard the concept phrased like this: "Who am I to judge?" or "You can't fight this wickedness. God has ordained this for the last days."

The fruit of this concept, no matter how it is verbalized, is un-involvement, retreat, and non-confrontation. This concept is not humility. It is instead arrogant and idolatrous, because it is a proclamation of a "make-believe truth" contrary to God's Word.

SATANIC HUMILITY

Silent consent to evil is not humility. God's Word shows us the proper way to face evil, and it is not retreat or isolation.

Better is open rebuke than love that is concealed.

Proverbs 27:5 (NASB)

Look, it does not say, "Better is love that is concealed than open rebuke." Neither does it say, "Better is private criticism than open rebuke." Nor does it say, "Better is acceptance than open rebuke." It just says, "BETTER IS OPEN REBUKE THAN LOVE THAT IS CONCEALED."

You see, the association with open rebuke is love. Maybe someone else's kids can play in the street but not yours. Why? You love your kids. Of course you will openly rebuke them if they are doing something dangerous to themselves. That IS love.

In the same way, God loves people and wants us to openly rebuke lies and deception that destroys millions. Their destruction is not just for a year or 75 years, but for eternity.

The following are lyrics from a song I wrote:

MORE COURAGE and LOVE

Don't ruffle feathers as though that was mean
You don't want to make a … scene
People in bondage and they don't even know it
You know the truth and don't … show it

Your righteousness can make some tense
You don't want to … offend
So you don't take a stand or raise your voice
As though you had … no choice

Call it "manners"; call it "nice"
When you are kind to sins and lies
But if you love God, you'll have to change
And call on yourself for more courage and love

Money gets all the attention,
Hearts crying out for affection
So many lives in the wrong direction
Where is God? Who can say?
You know God is the way
Where is your courage and love?

People dying on your left and your right
All you can be is … polite
Selling their souls just to find more light
You're silent because you are … shy

Call it "manners"; call it "nice"
When you are kind to sins and lies
But if you love God, you'll have to change
And call on yourself for more courage and love

It is final. We cannot be manipulated or restrained by political correctness. We cannot be taken aback when someone suggests we have poor manners or that we are judgmental. "Nice" is not our objective. "Obedience" to God and scripture is our objective. Being impolite or rude is not a worthy goal either. But do not be manipulated by a few words that intentionally make you silent.

Put Jesus here in our day and culture. People would find his uncompromising love offensive and judgmental. Even though he genuinely loves He would not be called "nice". At the very least, nice people might say Jesus had poor manners, according to the way most folks define these terms. We must look beyond the words and look toward spiritual objectives.

SIN—A RESPECTABLE ALTERNATIVE

Withholding restoration is never love. Even though many call God's truth "condemning" or "judgmental", it is God's truth that releases people from the sentence of condemnation.

Many Christians avoid speaking His truth so they will not hurt someone's feelings, like a doctor who doesn't want to tell a patient they have a serious condition. That's bad news. But the good news is that there is a cure. If there is no cure for sin or external condemnation, let's not spread the bad news. But if there is forgiveness, if there is truth, if there is a loving God, if there is healing and restoration . . . what are we waiting for?

God's Word puts it this way:

> Brethren, if a man be overtaken in a fault, ye which are spiritual, restore such a one in the spirit of meekness.
>
> **Galatians 6:1 (KJV)**

We are never to look down on anyone. We are all sinners. Not just "them"—us too. Those of us, who are saved, are saved by grace. God's justice would surely and fairly condemn us, but His mercy through Jesus redeems us from our guilt.

But while God is striving to save men from their sin, some Christians refuse to "judge".

> Be merciful, just as your Father is merciful. And do not judge and you will not be judged; and do not condemn, and you will not be condemned; pardon, and you will be pardoned.
>
> **Luke 6:36-38 (NASB)**

Truly, who are we to look down on anyone as if we are better? We are forgiven through mercy so we are wrong to look at someone else, shake our head, and condemn them as though they can never repent. We must look for opportunities for them to turn their life around, not assume they are forever dead in their sins.

Many preach that we should leave sinners alone in their sin but they don't say "leave them alone in their sin", that would be obviously wrong and it sounds clearly wrong. What we hear is "we are all sinners and we should not judge". It brings us to that obviously wrong conclusion but these words sound "wise and kind". Although the words sound right, if we are accepting sinfulness as a permanent status of all that sin—it is wrong. But what is far more common in our society is the idea of "live and let live", as if there is no real right or wrong. Whatever anyone does is a "respectable alternative". God says this attitude is wrong. I hope you are getting this. It's a little tricky but this is important for you to understand.

> Do not judge according to appearance, but judge with righteous judgment.
>
> **John 7:24 (NASB)**

What? Is God telling us to judge? Yes, in a discerning way. It is not a smart person who doesn't see any difference between right and wrong, good and bad, poison and nutritious, sweet and sour, life and death.

Because a person is charming, good-looking, or rich does not mean their conduct or ideas are OK.

God's values and truth must be openly proclaimed and certainly not kept secret. Satan wants God's truth hidden. We are polite to Satan and rude to God when we courteously withhold the truth about sin; the truth of how it brings bondage and various other serious consequences. God does not tell us that overlooking sin will restore a man. God tells us to "restore" the man "overtaken by a fault."

It is God's purpose to let His truth shine in the hearts of all men through us, even though we ourselves are saved sinners.

> You are the light of the world. A city set on a hill cannot be hidden. Nor do men light a lamp, and put it under the peck-measure, but on the lampstand; and it gives light to all who are in the house. Let your light shine before men in such a way that they may see your good works, and glorify your Father who is in heaven.
>
> **Matthew 5:14-16 (NASB)**

Mercy is not a basket that hides the light. God is not honored by those whose so-called mercy renders His truth useless.

What is more useless, more fruitless, and more hypocritical than the advice that Christians stay out of morally controversial arenas? Do you realize individual Christians know better than anyone else—what is right and what is wrong? Only people who seek God, study His Word, and believe His Word know the hope of truth. The ungodly lack real understanding of hope or truth, especially people with a selfish agenda.

> Evil men do not understand justice, but those who seek the LORD understand all things.
>
> **Proverbs 28:5 (NASB)**

Selfish men can only lead us into a pit, according to scripture. They are not guided by the Light. We are not smarter than other people, God surely is. We are not better humans than others; it is simply that His Word gives us direction. This is not an opinion of mine or even church doctrine, but pure Bible.

None of us know where all roads lead but with a map, we have insight on where the roads go and we can make much better choices. The Bible is that map.

CHRISTLIKE UNBELIEVERS AND PAGAN CHRISTIANS

Religious words do not equal a righteous life. Reader, please do not misread my meaning here. I would much prefer to model my life after a pagan who follows God's Word, even unconsciously, than a "church person" who continually ignores God's Word by his actions. I would not want a judge or a policeman to make decisions based on not offending people, even if he or she does go to church.

Many believers fear public opinion. It is never good for any of us to fear people more than God; that is to say, to be more concerned about what people think than motivated by our concern to do what God thinks.

> The fear of man brings a snare, But he who trusts in the LORD will be exalted. Many seek the ruler's favor, But justice for man comes from the LORD.
>
> **Proverbs 29:25-26 (NASB)**

Isn't it better to obey God than "believe" and then not obey? Be wary of folks that flaunt the name of God or Jesus but do not serve Him. What is the moral of the following parable Jesus told the Pharisees?

> But what do you think?
>
> A man had two sons, and he came to the first and said, "Son, go work today in the vineyard." And he answered and said, "I will, sir"; and he did not go. And he came to the second and said the same thing. But he answered and said, "I will not"; yet he afterward regretted it and went.
>
> Which of the two did the will of his father?
>
> They said, "The latter."

> Jesus said to them, "Truly I say to you that the tax-gatherers and harlots will get into the kingdom of God before you.
>
> **Matthew 21:28-31 (NASB)**

"Oh yeah, God is good. Let's do God's Will. I am a Christian. God bless you." That may be what he says, but what does he do? Pay more attention to life and actions than words. Actions reveal what men really believe.

"I don't trust Christians. Let's not get religious. I am not a Christian." If this man says that but helps the poor, stands against moral evil, loves courageously, he is a far better servant to God than the religious hypocrite. It was religious hypocrites that angered Jesus, not sinners. This man may not even be aware that he is pleasing to the Lord.

I know there are many good people like these Jesus told us a story about:

> For I was hungry, and you gave Me [something] to eat; I was thirsty, and you gave Me drink; I was a stranger, and you invited Me in; naked, and you clothed Me; I was sick, and you visited Me; I was in prison, and you came to Me.
>
> Then the righteous will answer Him, saying, "Lord, when did we see You hungry, and feed You, or thirsty, and give You drink? And when did we see You a stranger, and invite You in, or naked, and clothe You? And when did we see You sick, or in prison, and come to You?"
>
> And the King will answer and say to them,
>
> "Truly I say to you, to the extent that you did it to one of these brothers of Mine, even the least of them, you did it to Me."
>
> **Matthew 25:35-40 (NASB)**

The benefit of God's precepts is in the *doing* of those precepts. Real God-fearing people can judge in law and govern better, BUT ONLY if those people adhere to God's Word, regardless of its ramifications or unpopularity, first in their own lives, then in all other arenas. It takes wisdom, courage, and diligence.

WATCH THE WORDS AND PHRASES

There is a way that polls can be manipulated based on the wording of the questions. For example: *Should we allow abortions after 6 months or just up to 6 months?*

This allows no objection to abortion; it merely specifies how it should be legal.

Here is another example: *Should pornography be legal for those under 18 if they are married?*

Again, there is no option to object to pornography.

Here's another: *Should the Ten Commandments be banned from all public events or just those related to government and organizations with public funding?*

We are often put in the position of having to make a choice between two evils. We need to think beyond what manipulators are placing before us. We need to think.

For instance, in the much broader sense, it is not whether we will lovingly tolerate sin or hatefully not tolerate sin. Don't be misled by these false limited choices: *"Love people as they are" or "be a religious bigot and judge others".*

Wow, what a choice. Either love people by accepting everything they do or be a narrow-minded hateful bigot. Who wants to be a narrow-minded hateful bigot? So we cave and say to ourselves we want to be loving and accepting. Are these the only two options? Some would like you to think so. That is why it is worded this way. These are carefully constructed words to misguide.

Here is a better way to phrase your options:

"Silently watch people be destroyed by their sin" or "love them enough to show them a better way."

Doesn't that totally change your feeling about your options? Be very careful about how the media, polls, and people force you into a very limited choice. It is constructed to say if you don't agree with them, you are evil.

"Are you for allowing women to decide what they want to do with their own bodies, or do you think the government should control their bodies?" Is this really the issue? Again, I am being misdirected to only two bad options.

How about I rephrase it: *"Are you for encouraging women to hire people to kill their children while injuring them, the mothers, emotionally and possibly physically"*, or *"Do you think we should have laws saying this is wrong?"*

Amazingly, both of these sets of questions are the exact same subject but worded differently. Every American woman is already allowed to control her own body. She can use contraceptives. She can abstain from sex. It is illegal to force her to become pregnant against her will.

Her child within her is ANOTHER body and is already under the protection of the law. If someone killed her baby against her will it would be declared murder. She is alive but her baby is dead. How is this murder? Simple, her child is dead, not her own body. Is this just a political opinion?

The question is posed *"So you want women to go back to dark alleys at great risk of bleeding to death in order to get an illegal abortion?"*

Gee, I don't think that is what I want at all. I want literally millions of lives saved, which translates to millions of boys and girls. I want women NOT killing their own children and not having that on their conscience all their life. Close to half of these millions of babies are baby girls. I think I am more for women's rights than those demanding the "right" to destroy unborn baby girls.

This would add millions of taxpayers to the Social Security base. If you say they may be welfare babies it is a whole different discussion about killing the poor. No matter how you twist it, it is an unjust death sentence on an innocent human American life.

Permit me to abandon the issue of abortion and return to the larger point here.

Don't be more distracted by the questions or the controversy than the truth of scripture. We live in a dark land dominated by deception in many arenas. We have to think beyond the words put before us and add our own insight.

The choices are NOT "Shall we lovingly tolerate sin" or "hatefully not tolerate sin?"

Do not be misled by the manipulation of words to deceive you, people of God. Let's add the truth to the two limited choices that are both disobedience to God. Here it is:

We are called to, lovingly, not tolerate sin.

We are called to, lovingly, *not* merely standby while our fellow man is being destroyed. We are not to hate our fellow man, but rather help him when he is lost. We can tell—and it's even better if we can show—and help him.

We have not been called to fit pleasantly into the world and be "nice folks" endorsing rebellion against God. We have been called to win the world to God's holy alternative and overcome sin.

CHAPTER NINE

✧ ✧ ✧

Redeeming Love

God is never against sinners, nor are we if we are in His Will. God is saving sinners–like us, and we are called to continue the work. We must bring God's love and God's truth to those within and outside the church. We must speak clearly in loving confrontation first to ourselves, then to our families, and our fellow believers in error; and we must speak out even more clearly in the community, to create an atmosphere conducive to truth for the good of the whole community. The Ten Commandments is good for all societies. To withdraw and hide the truth is to fail God and His mandates for us.

A world without truth and against God is a very dark place. We are the light of the world.

> You are the light of the world. A city set on a hill cannot be hidden.
>
> **Matthew 5:14 (NASB)**

OBEDIENCE IS THE ONLY TRUE HUMILITY

There is nothing humble about apathy, laziness, or a lack of concern for the souls of men, women, and children in this generation. We may hear "Who am I to judge" but there is nothing humble about disobeying God's call to let our light shine for the sake of our fellow man.

We are to be a reflection of God's character and values in this generation so dominated by zealous ungodliness. We are the guiding light to those who do not know the reality of God's love and Jesus Christ. How can we expect to live without confrontation? To live without confrontation is sheer compromise in these times.

We don't have to go looking for trouble. Just take an uncompromising stand and the trouble will come to you. When that trouble comes it is God's way of publishing His truth and you must not pull back. Don't hide.

THE LOG IN YOUR EYE

Finger-pointing is not automatic righteousness. Here is that scripture again:

> And why do you look at the speck that is in your brother's eye, but do not notice the log that is in your own eye? Or how can you say to your brother, "Brother, let me take out the speck that is in your eye," when you yourself do not see the log that is in your own eye? You hypocrite, first take the log out of your own eye, and then you will see clearly to take out the speck that is in your brother's eye.
>
> **Luke 6:41-42 (NASB)**

The primary front that Christians need to attack first is their own turf. If it is holiness we want then it is our own sin we must attack first.

Please, there are two things I strongly encourage Christians to avoid which are on opposite ends of the spectrum: Self-righteousness and unworthiness.

First, do not attack the sins of others and exaggerate their evilness to minimize your own sins. We think of our own sins as "just being human". You may consider your sin "normal sin". What is normal sin? There is no normal sin. The wages of sin is death. All sin leads to death. Self-righteousness angered Christ, and to see Christ is to see the Father. Our own sins are always biblically just as bad, just as awful, and just as deadly as any other sin. Remember, Christ displayed the most emotional anger at religious hypocrisy. Our flag is love, not finger-pointing.

FEELING UNWORTHY

Having sinned does not disqualify your right to speak out. On the opposite end of self-righteousness is feeling unworthy because of your sins. This is the other trick played on us. This is why millions of believers have no moral influence. They feel unqualified. They feel they don't have the right to say that anything is wrong, especially if they've ever committed the same sin. We are so conscious, or someone makes us conscious, of our own sin, we feel we have no right to condemn any sin.

Guess what? No one has the "right" to condemn sin. We have no rights. It isn't about rights. Only a fool would want the right to condemn, especially if he understands, "... and forgive us our debts as we forgive our debtors". A loving servant of God, on the other hand, is duty-bound to warn others about sin and what a grievous error it is to pursue sin as a goal. We have all sinned; we simply want to save those people we care about from the inevitable consequences of their wrong choices. When we refuse to warn others we fail to love altogether. We refuse to help. We refuse to warn people that their destiny is certain harm. How is that love? It is not. It is the opposite of love. When we refuse to condemn sin—WE SIN. The more we refuse to speak up, the more we keep piling sins upon ourselves. More and more lives headed for fatal cliffs go right past us as we give them a friendly wave, knowing they are destined to fall headlong into a perilous canyon. Friends, this is a great unkindness.

THE LOG IN THE CHURCH'S EYE

Church folks are not necessarily good folks.

In churches we prefer to talk about the evil unbelievers while excusing or winking at the sin among church members. We are the "OK group" and those outside are not OK.

Paul makes the point for us to not associate with immoral people. Interestingly, he stresses the point that he is not referring to those sinners outside the church but rather the immoral within the church. God never intended for us to completely avoid immoral people by retreating to some Christian commune, clique, or denomination. How can we stop those people from walking off cliffs if we simply leave the area? We are called to lovingly mix it up with the unbelievers. Like Jesus did. He was invited to parties but He was a Light wherever He went. He didn't blend in anywhere. He was God's Will walking among us but in a very natural way. Of course, we should be ourselves and let that light of Christ shine through. There is nothing polite about hiding the glory of God in our hearts. There is nothing polite about pretending we agree with dishonesty in the workplace to blend in. And as already stated, it is not courtesy to be silent when our friends are cruising for disastrous peril.

There is no scripture inspiring us to judge just the unbelievers. We invented that. We are called to love unconditionally.

It is the sin within the church that we must first attack, and again, not the people. But Paul says to avoid those calling themselves Christians who simultaneously are sinning with no intention of repentance. There are so many people that look you straight in the face and say, "I'm not sinning" and explain that you are the one with a judging problem. If possible, Paul wants us to remove people such as this from the church. Sounds judgmental, does it not?

> I wrote you in my letter not to associate with immoral people; I [did] not at all [mean] with the immoral people of this

world, or with the covetous and swindlers, or with idolaters; for then you would have to go out of the world. But actually, I wrote to you not to associate with any so-called brother if he should be an immoral person, or covetous, or an idolater, or a reviler, or a drunkard, or a swindler—not even to eat with such a one. For what have I to do with judging outsiders? Do you not judge those who are within [the church]? But those who are outside, God judges. Remove the wicked man from among yourselves.

1 Corinthians 5:9-13 (NASB)

I hope you didn't miss a single word of that. You'd better read it again to make sure.

According to Peter, here is our real battle:

Beloved, I urge you as aliens and strangers to abstain from fleshly lusts, which wage war against the soul. Keep your behavior excellent among the Gentiles, so that in the thing in which they slander you as evildoers, they may on account of your good deeds, as they observe [them], glorify God in the day of visitation. Submit yourselves for the Lord's sake to every human institution, whether to a king as the one in authority, or to governors as sent by him for the punishment of evildoers and the praise of those who do right. For such is the will of God that by doing right you may silence the ignorance of foolish men. [Act] as free men, and do not use your freedom as a covering for evil, but [use it] as bondslaves of God. Honor all men; love the brotherhood, fear God, honor the king.

1 Peter 2:11-17 (NASB)

I ought to memorize this whole scripture. It says so much.

Christians, you and me, are to judge between right and wrong.

Christians, you and me, are to condemn sin.

Christians, you and me, are to fight wickedness, for God has ordained this for every generation of believers that serves Him.

We have a lifelong battle fighting the sin in ourselves.

We have a lifelong battle fighting the sin so prevalent within the churches.

We are not called to judge the unbelievers, but we are called to judge/discern what is right and what is wrong.

We are not called to condemn other Christians, but we are to judge sin and deal with it within the church. This is not my opinion; we are just studying what the Bible says. Go back and look at the scriptures in this chapter. They are set apart so you can easily do that.

We are not called to ever do anything that is not motivated by genuine love. Often, only God knows our true heart in this regard.

See past the words that manipulate you into disobeying God. Close your eyes, trust God's Word as true, and see the truth—then practice it.

We can never be perfect but we can practice. The more we practice, the better we will get, but we must practice. Practice obedience. Practice love. Practice fighting sin and error, don't attack people. God loves all people. Ultimately, all people will be judged by God, not us.

Practice learning the truth.

> By this the children of God and the children of the devil are obvious: anyone who does not practice righteousness is not of God, nor the one who does not love his brother. For this is the message which you have heard from the beginning, that we should love one another;
>
> **1 John 3:10-12 (NASB)**

CHAPTER TEN

✦ ✦ ✦

Love Plus Knowledge and Truth

. . . We know that we all possess knowledge. Knowledge puffs up, but love builds up.

1 Corinthians 8:1 (NIV)

Later in that same letter Paul says:

If I have the gift of prophecy and can fathom all mysteries and all knowledge, and if I have a faith that can move mountains, but have not love, I am nothing.

1 Corinthians 13:2 (NIV)

I cannot possibly overemphasize God's, Jesus', and the entire scripture's emphasis on love. However, no Christian can think that Paul is declaring that prophecy, knowledge, and faith are worthless. He says without love, they are of no value. With love they are of great value. Look at the scripture again. He is simply conveying that all of God's gifts are futile without love. All sacrifice for the Lord is pointless if it fails His most basic and important command—to love.

"Teacher, which is the great commandment in the Law?"

And He said to him,"You shall love the Lord your God with all your heart, and with all your soul, and with all your mind.

"This is the great and foremost commandment.

"The second is like it, 'You shall love your neighbor as yourself.'

"On these two commandments depend the whole Law and the Prophets."

Matthew 22:38-40 (NASB)

Just as faith and prophecy are really important, so is knowledge. God is not against knowledge, but rather the sheer vanity of knowledge without love. He is against the misuse of all things, including knowledge. He is against all things lifted up higher than their rightful place and this too includes knowledge.

God encourages His people to get knowledge because of its merit.

Solomon, famous for his wisdom, had asked God for wisdom even though he could have asked for riches. This impressed God so much he gave wisdom to Solomon as described here:

I will do what you have asked. I will give you a wise and discerning heart, so that there will never have been anyone like you, nor will there ever be.

I Kings 3:12 (NIV)

God promised great wisdom to Solomon, so it is appropriate that I quote him just a few times from the Proverbs on knowledge. I have capitalized the word "KNOWLEDGE" for your benefit.

With his mouth the godless destroys his neighbor, but through KNOWLEDGE the righteous escape.

Proverbs 11:9 (NIV)

The fear of the LORD is the beginning of KNOWLEDGE; fools despise wisdom and instruction.

Proverbs 1:7 (NASB)

For the LORD gives wisdom; from His mouth come KNOWLEDGE and understanding.

Proverbs 2:6 (NASB)

Take my instruction, and not silver, and KNOWLEDGE rather than choicest gold.

Proverbs 8:10 (NASB)

Every prudent man acts with KNOWLEDGE, but a fool displays folly.

Proverbs 13:16 (NASB)

Part of wisdom is discerning what is true from what is not true. There is so much misinformation coming at us every day, and so little truth.

No matter how brilliant a person may be, if he is operating on a wrong premise, he will be bound by that wrong information. One may be an expert sharpshooter, but if he thinks he is supposed to shoot a deer in the antlers, he will turn out to be a flop as a deer hunter. He has the wrong target. He has the wrong goal. He has the wrong information.

God urges us to be wise as serpents and as gentle as doves.

Today we have seen the traditional "pursuit of happiness", a supporting pillar in our national laws, converted to "happily pursuing selfishness". The media, government, and mental health centers consider fornication, adultery, homosexuality, cheating, lying, and rebellion against God as normal behavior. Virginity, chastity, honesty, truth, and faith in Jesus are considered abnormal today. What kind of target is this? Teenagers continually submissive to their parents often arouse concern by teachers. "These 'victimized' children must have very controlling parents", they assume. Rebellious teenagers are considered more normal. Folks, this is not healthy.

Mental health has the objective of "normalizing" patients into healthy, happy, normal people. Unfortunately, if you don't conform to society's definition of normal, you are considered deranged. What are the implications here? Our current American culture has values reflected in its laws. Do you see a nation seeking the approval of God? No, our generation is largely embracing what God calls sinful conduct as normal, healthy living. Look at the results this has produced in our society. An "expert" witness could testify in a legal court and declare you, me, or our children in need of counseling because we are "abnormal".

Has God called each Christian generation to conform to their surrounding morality? Of course not.

> Woe to those who call evil good, and good evil; who substitute darkness for light and light for darkness; who substitute bitter for sweet, and sweet for bitter!
>
> **Isaiah 5:20 (NASB)**

> He who justifies the wicked, and he who condemns the righteous, both of them alike are an abomination to the LORD.
>
> **Proverbs 17:15 (NASB)**

> Woe to those who enact evil statutes, and to those who constantly record unjust decisions,
>
> **Isaiah 10:1 (NASB)**

This is all very relevant scripture. Obviously we are not to be chameleons that change to the color of our environment. What the world calls "normal", God may rightfully call "sinful". What is politically correct often changes several times during one lifetime. The Bible states it simply:

> Do not conform any longer to the pattern of this world, but be transformed by the renewing of your mind. Then you

will be able to test and approve what God's will is—
his good, pleasing and perfect will.

Romans 12:2 (NIV)

Note, God says, that you may PROVE what the Will of God is. If we are ignorant of the world around us and ignorant of God's Will how can we obey this command? Here we are back to knowledge again. If we don't understand the issues, how can we speak out? If we will not speak out, how can we prove the Will of God to our generation?

Listen as Isaiah echoes the words of Hosea. I have added italics for emphasis.

Therefore my people will go into exile for *lack of understanding;*
their men of rank will die of hunger and their masses will
be parched with thirst.

Isaiah 5:13 (NIV)

A lack of understanding . . . can be the cause leading to exile. That is a heavy sentence for just a lack of understanding. Have Jews been exiled? The sentence was clearly fulfilled for them several times.

I am sure the Israelites could not imagine another country ruling theirs before it happened. They heard of it happening to other countries but had never personally experienced it. Could it happen to us? Could Americans ever go into exile? Could the American dream of a Christian nation vanish?

It is happening right under our noses, with little protest. We are like the frogs boiled in water whose death comes comfortably because the temperature change is so gradual and unnoticeable.

Is it possible that we Christians in America may not even know the difference between right and wrong? If we compare 72 degrees to 71 degrees we are not concerned about the change. If we compare 93 degrees to 92 degrees we see no cause for alarm. But what if we compare something to an absolute? What if we decide that 70 degrees is "right"? 75 degrees is wrong. 90 degrees is wrong. 92 and 93 degrees are wrong. We need to get back to 70 degrees. With absolutes, we see how far we are from God's requirement for morality and righteousness. No wonder so many are against the very idea of absolutes. They intellectualize by making examples that make absolutes look ridiculous. For example, they will show how something unacceptable in our culture is completely acceptable in another country. Or they may present historical evidence of a nation or culture doing things and turn this into "normal" because someone somewhere did it a long time ago. As a matter of fact, I hear "human behavior" used as a gauge for "normal" all the time. There is a great deception that if enough people agree on something, it then becomes the truth. If we say it's OK, then it becomes OK.

We are sometimes like unthinking sheep when we do not want to look foolish. But we are foolish if we simply blend into our own culture. This would mean that believers in Europe think something is alright but believers in Africa consider something else acceptable that the European church disagrees with. Then, in the Scandinavian region it is morally acceptable to do things scandalous to both Africans and Europeans and on and on. We all read the same Bible. What is our comeback? Where are our examples of how it is foolish not believing absolutes?

Nature and science are filled with absolutes even though some use it differently.

Once, while in college, a professor was telling my class that there were no absolutes. Naturally, I raised my hand and asked if he was *absolutely* sure. (This was something I had learned from Loren Cunningham.) He gave an example of how we believe gravity holds everything down but there were some Indian tribes that believed gravity held everything up. He smiled as my freshman classmates nodded in approval. I raised my hand again and when called upon said, "Whether we believe gravity holds everything down or up, *absolutely* nobody, including the animals, float away." He actually moved past the subject and I ended up with a bad grade in that class. Still, most of my classmates agreed with the professor because I was just a kid and he was a "doctor" teaching science. They assumed because of his age, education, and position that he must be right and I must be wrong to disagree. This is no different from our reaction to our society, the media, and the so-called norms of our time.

How will we learn the definition of God's righteousness, justice, and equity without studying the Bible? We cannot even begin without truth.

There is an abundance of Bibles throughout our nation, yet there is a greater abundance of ignorance of what the Bible is telling God's people. Worse yet, there are theologians and Bible scholars that "swallow a camel while straining at a gnat" regarding the scriptures. They render God's truth ineffective by taking obvious truth and turning it into sophisticated doctrine that few completely understand. Surely our ignorance will not have a blissful ending. Can we expect a different punishment from the God, who is the same yesterday, today, and forever?

Remember Christians, ignorance is not bliss, but the path to exile according to Isaiah 5:13. Wisdom is the opposite of ignorance. Why would any good person not want to pursue understanding, wise behavior, righteousness, justice, and equity? God intends for us to obtain these qualities and will help us.

> The proverbs of Solomon son of David, king of Israel: for attaining wisdom and discipline; for understanding words of insight; for acquiring a disciplined and prudent life, doing what is right and just and fair; for giving prudence to the simple, knowledge and discretion to the young–let the wise listen and add to their learning, and let the discerning get guidance
>
> **Proverbs 1:1-5 (NASB)**

How can we lead the naive away from the ignorance that is so devastating; by silence, by apathy, by letting the ungodly give *their* reasons for *their* convictions while we remain silent? Can we do it by letting anti-God, anti-Bible sympathizers or amoral people write, establish, and enforce most laws in our nation?

The personage of Wisdom speaks in Chapter 1:22-32 in Proverbs.

In this scripture you will see the question from Wisdom wondering why believers prefer to be ignorant when Wisdom has so much promise. Wisdom, in this portion of scripture, will tell the future of those who don't bother getting it. The outcome for those who learn wisdom but ignore it is just as severe. Trouble is coming for any and all who miss, ignore, or disobey Wisdom. Trouble is unavoidable. Ultimately, people tend to try altering the very definition of truth to justify their foolishness and the trouble in their life. At that point, if they go looking for the truth they can't even find it. This scripture says if they go looking for Wisdom, it will ignore them and allow them to be destroyed for spurning the truth, Wisdom, and God. They will reap all the consequences of foolishness because that is what they chose instead of wisdom. It is all here. Read it for yourself.

> How long will you simple ones love your simple ways? How long will mockers delight in mockery and fools hate knowledge? If you had responded to my rebuke, I would have poured out my heart to you and made my thoughts known to you. But since you rejected me when I called and no one gave heed when I stretched out my hand, since you ignored all my advice and would not accept my rebuke, I in turn will laugh at your disaster; I will mock when calamity overtakes you–when calamity overtakes you like a storm, when disaster sweeps over you like a whirlwind, when distress and trouble overwhelm you. Then they will call to me but I will not answer; they will look for me but will not find me. Since they hated knowledge and did not choose to fear the LORD, since they would not accept my advice and spurned my rebuke, they will eat the fruit of their ways and be filled with the fruit of their schemes. For the waywardness of the simple will kill them, and the complacency of fools will destroy them;
>
> **Proverbs 1:22-32 (NIV)**

Hopefully, you read every word in that passage carefully. If not, please read it again. It is Wisdom's warning.

Please notice that naiveté is not portrayed as a state of innocence. No, instead naiveté is presented as waywardness. Waywardness is defiance, disobedience, or rebellion. Does that surprise you? At the same time, Wisdom offers reproof and correction, but fools hate it. They will defend their foolishness or waywardness by justifying it somehow. Foolishness wants recognition, credit and praise, not correction. It is bent on being right more than getting right.

More importantly, Wisdom tells us that there is no excuse for ignorance. If we choose to remain ignorant and actually avoid learning wisdom, we shall eat the fruit of our own way. If we remain apathetic to the corruption around us, our complacency as fools will destroy us. While there is still time we must act or, like it happens in a human lifetime, the time will come when seeking Wisdom is too late. Read it for yourself again. Wisdom will then mock us when our calamity comes. We will prove Wisdom was right because we did not heed and calamity did come just as Wisdom promised.

In the very next verse, Wisdom tells us:

> but whoever listens to me will live in safety and be at ease,
> without fear of harm.
>
> **Proverbs 1:33 (NIV)**

Ah, what a great promise; a lesson worth understanding.

As the godless in our society continue to impose their own morality on everyone, they accuse pro-God types of trying to bring into legislation "radical" morality. We don't see the constant double standard while they point fingers and constantly keep doing what they accuse us of doing or trying to do. They make everyone afraid of us forcing our beliefs on others while they consistently continue forcing their beliefs on everyone.

We naively hide in our churches praying the ungodly will somehow do the Will of God and share the true knowledge that we personally lack? This might be funny if it wasn't so tragic.

We must know the truth ourselves, publicize it in an understandable manner to our family, friends, and in whatever arena God brings us to. This is the Will of God.

In our particular country, America, God has provided us with an opportunity to rule . . . no, it is an *invitation* to rule, because of our knowledge. No, it is even more than an invitation because He promises terrible consequences if we disobey. We are COMMANDED to obey God in every arena He gives us. We are to always stand for righteousness and against unrighteousness with hearts of love. It is the calling and duty of every Christian in every generation, according to scripture.

How beautiful that God is making wisdom, knowledge, and truth available to His people. Whatever our reasons may be for rejecting this knowledge and wisdom, the devastating consequences will be the same. This truth is repeated over and over throughout the Bible.

We know it is not only for our own sake that we need to know what is true and right, but also so we openly proclaim truth, contradicting what is false and wrong, in an attitude of love and meekness. We are God's people and we are and must be the salt of the earth, we are and must be the light of the world. We must not be apathetic or "complacent as the fools" of whom Wisdom speaks. Love would not permit it. We must be knowledgeable and always ready to give the true and right answer.

Here is a verse in two translations; the New American Standard Bible and the New International Version.

> but sanctify Christ as Lord in your hearts, always being ready to make a defense to every one who asks you to give an account for the hope that is in you, yet with gentleness and reverence;
>
> **1 Peter 3:15 (NASB)**

> But in your hearts set apart Christ as Lord. Always be prepared to give an answer to everyone who asks you to give the reason for the hope that you have. But do this with gentleness and respect,
>
> **1 Peter 3:15 (NIV)**

This information I am giving you is biblical knowledge. His Word is knowledge and wisdom. True knowledge is very important. Learn it. Believe it. Practice it with love. Like all of the commandments, the knowledge of truth is the pre-cursor of action. In other words, obedience is the trigger of reward.

CHAPTER ELEVEN

✦ ✦ ✦

The Prophets

> Blessed are the peacemakers, for they shall be called sons of God.
>
> **Matthew 5:9 (NASB)**

Many Christians believe it is un-Christian to confront issues. They shrink into an almost secret Christian life and claim to be peacemakers instead of troublemakers. Is this the peace-making Jesus blessed? For starters, let us consider any prophet in the Bible, including Jesus. Let us examine if they modeled for us a silent pacifism with secret convictions or if their convictions were public.

THE PROPHET HOSEA

Found in the book of Hosea is record of the prophet's words to people in his own community. If a man said these same words to Christians in America, would he become popular or unpopular? Listen to Hosea the prophet.

> There is only cursing, lying and murder, stealing and adultery; they break all bounds, and bloodshed follows bloodshed.

> Because of this the land mourns, and all who live in it waste away; the beasts of the field and the birds of the air and the fish of the sea are dying. "But let no man bring a charge, let no man accuse another, for your people are like those who bring charges against a priest. You stumble day and night, and the prophets stumble with you. So I will destroy your mother--my people are destroyed from lack of knowledge. Because you have rejected knowledge, I also reject you as my priests; because you have ignored the law of your God, I also will ignore your children.
>
> **Hosea 4:2-6 (NIV)**

Hosea is talking to God's people! He is telling God's people they are guilty of these atrocities. Further, he is warning them of the grave punishments to come. Hosea is judging the people and their conduct. He is confronting them. He is fighting the wickedness of his day. Is Hosea a peacemaker? Yes. He wants these people to see, with clarity, their sin. Sin is always wrong. Sin is always a mistake. Repentance from wrong to right is the biblical way to make peace with God and the common sense way to correct what is wrong. God desires to forgive us—but cannot forgive sins we refuse to give up.

Through Hosea, God is pleading with His chosen people, Israel. He loves them and knows the consequences of their sinfulness. He will forgive them if they repent. He will judge them, and rightly so, if they continue in their sin. From the text, we can see that God's people have rejected knowledge, and due to their lack of knowledge, they are destroyed. In loving confrontation Hosea reflects God's concern and beckons the people of Israel to return to understanding and righteousness. If repentance results from understanding Hosea's words, God's truth will set them free.

Is it not more loving to call people to repentance than to "mercifully" ignore their sins, or worse yet, to justify or excuse their sins? Is this who God wants to bless as peacemakers?

Throughout history God has used prophets to call His people to righteousness. To lead the people to repentance, prophets have always had to "tell things as they really are". Prophets avoided euphemisms and even what some may call "tact". They simply called things by their right name. Sin is still sin; murder is still murder; adultery is still adultery; idolatry is still idolatry. These words have brought death to many of the prophets because people hate being told that what they are doing is wrong. It is as though softer words will ease the consequences of our error, but of course that is nonsense. Prophets bring God's light but usually people love darkness rather than light. None the less prophets, God's own messengers, continue to preach God's Word without flinching.

Sadly, much of the "hard" preaching we hear is not to the sinners in the church. Instead, audiences that pay to hear their preacher talk, hear about how sinful the world outside is. We huddle in our own Christian cliques and talk about the awfulness of sin in the world, but this is not the ministry the prophets had. If it were, they would have never been persecuted. God usually sent them to His own people, although not always, and it was usually God's own people that persecuted and killed the prophets.

How well would the following words go if directed to a group of religious leaders today?

> Woe to you, scribes and Pharisees, hypocrites! For you build the tombs of the prophets and adorn the monuments of the righteous, and say, "If we had been [living] in the days of our fathers, we would not have been partners with them in [shedding] the blood of the prophets." Consequently you bear witness against yourselves, that you are sons of those who murdered the prophets. Fill up then the measure [of the guilt] of your fathers. You serpents, you brood of vipers, how shall you escape the sentence of hell? Therefore, behold, I am sending you prophets and wise men and scribes; some of them you will kill and crucify, and some of them you will scourge in your synagogues, and persecute from city to city, that upon you may fall [the guilt of] all the righteous blood shed on earth, from the blood of righteous Abel to the blood of Zechariah, the son of Berechiah, whom you murdered between the temple and the altar. Truly I say to you, all these things shall come upon this generation.

Matthew 23:29-36 (NASB)

These were the words of Jesus to the religious leaders of His day and most of them hated Him for that. Surely, Jesus doesn't need counsel on how to tactfully approach problems. We cannot rebuke Jesus Himself for doing a poor job of recruiting support for His ministry. The disciples could see how Jesus was "ruining" the potential of His ministry by losing the religious leaders' support. Jesus is above all, the very model of living out God's Will in our sinful world.

Please don't miss the point that it was sin IN THE CHURCH that Jesus confronted and it was CHURCH LEADERS that had Him killed.

THE PROPHET MALACHI

Malachi was another prophet of the Lord. Like most of us, he was no stranger in his community, nor was he a popular speaker. No one invited him to dinner groups to speak on issues. No one invited him to unfold his opinions.

As a boy, he must have had his own childhood dreams of following in his father's career; a normal thing in his day.

Malachi had to grow up as we all do and as he matured into manhood, he witnessed the increase of corruption in his community. Not only was Malachi grieved with the situation, but God showed the man His perspective of this corruption.

Is that corruption much different from modern America where nearly everyone's credibility is in question?

In God's picture of corruption to Malachi, the Lord showed His diagnosis of the problem, the Divine method of cure, the judgment that awaits those who cannot be cured; and His broken heart for His wayward people. Malachi must have praised God as he realized the Lord's redemptive motivation in condemning sin.

When Malachi stepped out and showed God's perspective on people's conduct, undoubtedly Malachi lost some close friends. More than likely members of Malachi's own family, possibly even his in-laws, were against his proclamations of God's Word since he was disapproving of what was culturally approved. The prophet's own career plans must have been altered considerably when he obeyed God and spoke out against the corruption of his day. Picture the expressions of the people when Malachi looked them in the eye and said,

> Another thing you do: You flood the LORD's altar with tears. You weep and wail because he no longer pays attention to your offerings or accepts them with pleasure from your hands. You ask, "Why?" It is because the LORD is acting as the witness between you and the wife of your youth, because you have broken faith with her, though she is your partner, the wife of your marriage covenant. Has not [the LORD] made them one? In flesh and spirit they are his. And why one? Because he was seeking godly offspring. So guard yourself in your spirit, and do not break faith with the wife of your youth. "I hate divorce," says the LORD God of Israel,"and I hate a man's covering himself with violence as well as with his garment," says the LORD Almighty. So guard yourself in your spirit, and do not break faith. You have wearied the LORD with your words. "How have we wearied him?" you ask. By saying, "All who do evil are good in the eyes of the LORD, and he is pleased with them" or "Where is the God of justice?"
>
> **Malachi 2:13-17 (NIV)**

Here is the same scripture in the New American Standard Version

> And this is another thing you do: you cover the altar of the LORD with tears, with weeping and with groaning, because He no longer regards the offering or accepts [it with] favor from your hand. Yet you say, "For what reason?" Because the LORD has been a witness between you and the wife of your youth, against whom you have dealt treacherously, though she is your companion and your wife by covenant. But not one has done [so] who has a remnant of the Spirit. And what did [that] one [do] while he was seeking a godly offspring? Take heed then, to

> your spirit, and let no one deal treacherously against the wife of your youth. For I hate divorce," says the LORD, the God of Israel, and him who covers his garment with wrong," says the LORD of hosts. So take heed to your spirit, that you do not deal treacherously. You have wearied the LORD with your words. Yet you say, "How have we wearied Him" In that you say, "Everyone who does evil is good in the sight of the LORD, and He delights in them," or, "Where is the God of justice?"
>
> **Malachi 2:13-17 (NASB)**

Can you picture the people patting Malachi on the back saying, "You're a splendid prophet", or do you find it easier to imagine people scorning Malachi and despising his words?

Can you hear his relatives comment about him, shaking their heads embarrassed and angry? Or can you see someone saying, "Malachi, you are making people feel miserable and guilty. Why don't you just go home"?

Have we, in the USA, wearied the Lord with our words? Do we call evil "good"? Do we call good "evil"?

Will we Christians in America continue to alienate ourselves from political responsibility, while wringing our hands over the injustice all around us? Will we rush from person to person to play the "isn't it awful" game and continue failing to raise our hands to stop this evil?

Are we much different from the people Malachi spoke to, or are we more righteous?

Seriously, what if you were confronted in public with your sin, would you repent or would you prefer to have that prophet silenced? He is making you look bad confronting your sin in public.

What if we began to speak on things according to God's perspective and definition, do you think most people would congratulate us, or would we be despised? The answers are obvious.

IF NOT YOU—THEN WHO?

If God's people do not speak the truth of His Word, the multitudes are abandoned to the wrong assumptions they have. The propaganda and error offered by atheists, pagans, compromising believers now in high places, and through the media are the advice and values the masses are given every day.

What morality is being taught on the talk shows, in the movies, in the classroom, among peers, at the workplace, in magazines, and on the internet?

If knowing the truth is what sets people free, then conversely, it is lies that bring bondage. Before we even have a desire to escape bondage, we must see the difference between the truth and lies. If we desire the truth and want to escape bondage, then we must plan our escape from bondage–that plan is a plan of repentance. According to God, truth triggering repentance is the beginning of liberty.

> The Spirit of the Lord GOD is upon me, Because the LORD has anointed me To bring good news to the afflicted; He has sent me to bind up the brokenhearted, To proclaim liberty to captives, And freedom to prisoners;
>
> **Isaiah 61:1 (NASB)**

God yearns to afford everyone the opportunity to repent. He does this by illuminating them with the truth. Who will go if not His own people?

God allows each individual to decide whether he will respond positively to the truth, run from it, or try to compromise it. The only way to bring a person, a people, or a nation out of darkness is by proclaiming truth. Truth is the light. Truth is the medicine. Without truth, there is no hope of repentance.

> The Lord is not slow about His promise, as some count slowness, but is patient toward you, not wishing for any to perish but for all to come to repentance.
>
> **2 Peter 3:9 (NASB)**

Truth is not always pleasant, but it is always accurate.

A good doctor is not always pleasant. Sometimes surgery is required. The doctor has to cut deeply into the flesh. There may be much blood. It looks gruesome and violent. To an ignorant person, surgery would look like someone being brutally attacked with a knife. But surgery is sometimes the only way to save a life.

A good minister is not always pleasant. He must point out flaws in his flock, so they can repent and come closer to God.

A good Christian is obedient to God—whether called to fight, to forgive, to overcome, to lift up, to put down, or to be silent.

A pat on the back may always be desirable but it is always the wrong goal for one striving to always do right. Throughout history, God's people have been persecuted, mistreated, afflicted, tortured, and even killed. Popular acceptance from people has never been the goal of true saints through the centuries.

While we Christians have been trying to be popular, hip, and politically correct, we have become a stench in God's nostrils.

> Woe to you when all men speak well of you, for in the same way their fathers used to treat the false prophets.
>
> **Luke 6:26 (NASB)**

It is time we reviewed our values, our obligation, our responsibilities before God, and who it is we fear most, God or man.

Proverbs tells us:

> The fear of man brings a snare, but he who trusts in the LORD will be exalted.
>
> **Proverbs 29:25 (NASB)**

> The fear of the LORD is the beginning of wisdom, and knowledge of the Holy One is understanding.
>
> **Proverbs 9:10 (NIV)**

The fear of man leads to error. Charm may captivate, but God's truth liberates. What will be the ultimate consequence of pleasing man and displeasing God?

Exactly what has God called us to do? Scripturally it appears we must know, live, and speak the truth. We must be prophets in our own day. It was just as much of a sacrifice for the prophets in the Old Testament to speak the truth to their generation as it is for us in our own generation. Yet this is what Christians are called to do, to bear witness to the truth.

...For the testimony of Jesus is the spirit of prophecy.

Revelation 19:10b (NASB)

CHAPTER TWELVE

✦ ✦ ✦

Jesus–His Love Offends Religious Hypocrisy

I know of a believer who pointed his finger at some well-known church leaders in public and started calling them names. I even counted how many times he called them names—17 times, in front of everybody. How immature and rude is that?

Jesus was that name-caller. In one chapter, Matthew 23, He called the religious leaders derogatory names and insulted them 17 times in one confrontation. Jesus was clearly insulting these religious and community leaders. The same conduct would be condemned today by most people, churched or not, as unloving and rude. There was an awful cancer sucking the life out of the nation of Israel and Jesus was doing surgery.

Look at the tone of Jesus' words here as we review 15 name-calling instances from several chapters in Matthew—using only 7 different names; snakes, brood of vipers, hypocrites, blind guides, blind fools, blind men, blind Pharisee.

> But when he saw many of the Pharisees and Sadducees coming to where he was baptizing, he said to them: "You brood of vipers! Who warned you to flee from the coming wrath?"
>
> **Matthew 3:7 (NIV)**

You brood of vipers, how can you who are evil say anything good? For out of the overflow of the heart the mouth speaks.

Matthew 12:34 (NIV)

You snakes! You brood of vipers! How will you escape being condemned to hell?

Matthew 23:33 (NIV)

Woe to you, teachers of the law and Pharisees, you hypocrites! You shut the kingdom of heaven in men's faces. You yourselves do not enter, nor will you let those enter who are trying to. Woe to you, teachers of the law and Pharisees, you hypocrites! You travel over land and sea to win a single convert, and when he becomes one, you make him twice as much a son of hell as you are.

Matthew 23:13-15 (NIV)

Woe to you, teachers of the law and Pharisees, you hypocrites! You give a tenth of your spices; mint, dill and cumin. But you have neglected the more important matters of the law; justice, mercy and faithfulness. You should have practiced the latter, without neglecting the former.

Matthew 23:23 (NIV)

Woe to you, teachers of the law and Pharisees, you hypocrites! You clean the outside of the cup and dish, but inside they are full of greed and self-indulgence.

Matthew 23:25 (NIV)

In the same way, on the outside you appear to people as righteous but on the inside you are full of hypocrisy and wickedness.

Matthew 23:28 (NIV)

> Woe to you, blind guides! You say, "If anyone swears by the temple, it means nothing; but if anyone swears by the gold of the temple, he is bound by his oath. "You blind fools! Which is greater: the gold, or the temple that makes the gold sacred? You blind men! Which is greater: the gift, or the altar that makes the gift sacred?
>
> **Matthew 23:16-17, 19 (NIV)**

> You blind guides! You strain out a gnat but swallow a camel.
>
> **Matthew 23:24 (NIV)**

> Blind Pharisee! First clean the inside of the cup and dish, and then the outside also will be clean.
>
> **Matthew 23:26 (NIV)**

Jesus seems mean and harsh. Why not talk to them privately with winsome tact?

It is so grave a misfortune when someone is finally ready to turn to God and the people they turn to are more religious than loving. Instead of finding the loving arms of God, new seekers may find in the religious leaders a burdensome load of religion. Instead of the love of God, His holiness, His mercy, and His truth—many are taught religious rules. Today folks are often exploited or manipulated by doctrine favoring a denomination, making them believe they have no access to God except through the so-called "true church"—the favored denomination—making Jesus Christ less important than the denomination and love less important than doctrine.

Dear reader, love *is* the true Bible doctrine. Too many professing church leaders talk to new believers or members of their denomination as though they, the leaders, are far more loved by God and that the others do not have the same access to God as they do.

Then Peter began to speak:

> I now realize how true it is that God does not show favoritism
>
> **Acts 10:34 (NIV)**

For God does not show favoritism.

Romans 2:11 (NIV)

God has no favorite church. He loves all people equally. Jesus died for people, not organizations. I am not saying all doctrine is equal. As I stated earlier, life based on truth sets free, lives based on lies bring bondage.

Religious leaders who are blind guides have an awful fate, according to scripture. If they are arrogant enough to publicly proclaim that the God of all mankind is sending everyone to hell who is not a member of their denomination, they deserve public denouncement by someone truly loving and truly representing God. Public deception needs public rebuke.

Can you begin to see the importance of love and courage in our generation? Who will stand for this generation? There is a war. Who is fighting?

We want revival; so does God. Men have notions that their plan is superior to God's. Think about this: The Bible clearly teaches one thing but we and some church leaders have a better idea. A better idea than God's wisdom? Yeah, all the time, this is nothing new. Peter figured crucifixion was a bad and unnecessary idea for Jesus. He thought Jesus had greater potential than death on a cross.

But when Jesus turned and looked at his disciples, he rebuked Peter. "Out of my sight, Satan!" he said. "You do not have in mind the things of God, but the things of men."

Mark 8:33 (NIV)

Our generation is being swallowed up without resistance. The honest, the righteous, they must speak out and replace sweet poison with life-giving truth for nourishment and life to the dying.

The lips of the righteous nourish many, but fools die for lack of judgment.

Proverbs 10:21 (NIV)

BIBLICAL LOVE

Let's look back to Jesus' time. We can easily see some intellectual drooling for a public debate with Jesus-this now famous carpenter-theologian from Nazareth. The Pharisees assume this man from Galilee cannot possibly compete with their intellectual wizardry with words. Puffed up with pride in their education, they are the kind of "foolosophers" who take glee in turning simple truth into a complicated mystery by asking all kinds of "deep" questions.

The Pharisees ask Jesus to define love, truth, or God. They love the war of words. The intellectual has rehearsed all the answers to anything Jesus might say. However, in His simple loving way, Jesus refuses the bait, and ends all controversy with these answers:

> Jesus answered, "I am the way and the truth and the life. No one comes to the Father except through me."
>
> **John 14:6 (NIV)**

Wow. All those long nights of intellectual discussions challenging every answer for undermining every claim of truth—there was no rehearsed answer or even a set-up question for an answer such as the one Jesus gave.

Jesus, rather than permit love or truth to degenerate into mere wordplay, held Himself up as the actual embodiment of love, truth, and life.

His life is the truth. His choices and actions reveal love and true life. Truth is no game of words.

Jesus Christ reflects the heart and character of God so accurately that He tells Philip, in another passage, that seeing Him (Jesus) is seeing God, the Father.

Jesus answered:

> "Don't you know me, Philip, even after I have been among you such a long time? Anyone who has seen me has seen the Father. How can you say, `Show us the Father'?"
>
> **John 14:9 (NIV)**

Do you see how ridiculous it is for us to preach one way and to live another? We can only reproduce what we are. If we are hypocrites, that is what we reproduce. How sad that folks calling us hypocrites may be more honest than we ourselves. It is *living* the truth that sets us free, and others too.

JESUS—OUR EXAMPLE OF LOVE

Now we will take a look at more scripture so that we can heed what Jesus tells us. We will use Him as our model for God and godliness. God is love.

The apostle John says there ain't no such thing as an unloving believer. He says the same person who doesn't love just plain doesn't know God.

> The one who does not love does not know God, for God is love.
>
> **1 John 4:8 (NASB)**

Am I accurate if I say that Jesus is love? If God is love and he who has seen Jesus has seen God, the Father, isn't Jesus also love?

We will use Jesus' life to model true love.

The scripture elevates one quality above all else, so highly that it becomes the mark of the believer. This quality is love. The Word says that love is from God and ONLY those who love are born of God. ONLY those who love can even know God.

> Dear friends, let us love one another, for love comes from God. Everyone who loves has been born of God and knows God.
>
> **1 John 4:7 (NIV)**

The quality "love", both verb and noun, is elevated to the highest possible pinnacle by equating it with God Himself.

> Whoever does not love does not know God, because God is love.
>
> **1 John 4:8 (NIV)**

GOD = LOVE JESUS = GOD JESUS = LOVE

We are not stretching any truth by presenting Jesus Christ as the best model for love and godliness. Let us examine the love of Jesus on a number of points that are seldom presented.

JESUS—HIS LOVE DIVIDES

Complacency rarely existed in the presence of Jesus. Jesus granted no one the luxury of delayed response since delayed obedience is disobedience.

A person might have justification for delaying obedience if there were vagueness or uncertainty. Therefore, Jesus would make the truth simple and evident to all. With truth laid out so plainly, there were only four options for the person whom He addressed:

1. To agree and submit to the truth.
2. To run from the truth.
3. To alter the truth.
4. To extinguish the truth.

As people gravitated to the options there was always a consequent assembling of sides bringing division, dissension, and confrontation.

There would have been more unity if there was ignorance, vagueness, uncertainty, or confusion. But Jesus brought clarity.

Truth today divides the same as it did in the days when Jesus trod the earth. Expect it.

DIMENSION IS NOT CONTRADICTION

This is worth understanding so please read carefully.

Jesus doesn't give us formulas. He gives us life. Life is truly three-dimensional. We so crave to simplify all of truth to a phrase or formula we can write on a wall. But the reality of life is "Love is the answer" that touches every single aspect of our life. How does love affect how I work, how I eat, my marriage, raising my children, dealing with people of other religions, and people who are dishonest, immoral, or violent?

Jesus offers His life not only on the cross but as an example of living. He shows us God's Will for us all. He literally came down from heaven and lived among us in a human body to not have an unfair edge as our model.

It takes a great deal of thinking, analyzing, and choices that seem contrary to our nature to walk out the things that we say we believe. In the Bible you find principles and statements that appear to be contradictory. Truth is not linear or two-dimensional. Like life, truth is three-dimensional.

There are many things that at first seem contradictory but are not. Gravity and aerodynamics may seem contradictory but aircraft are designed with careful regard to both of these scientific properties.

At first, judging something as wrong can be seen as the opposite of love. We have already explained how love and judging right from wrong are not contradictory but critically woven together. We want to know what our young children do wrong so we can protect them and teach them what is safe, true, and right; certainly not so we can judge them. Parents that don't know the difference between right and wrong, or those who let their children experiment because they refuse to judge them, are risking a charge of negligence.

Maybe you've heard the story of the three blind men. This is not a story from the Bible. It is a well-known story of three blind men who encountered an elephant. Each man was experiencing a different part of the elephant's anatomy. One felt the trunk, and another the ear, the third felt the tail. Naturally, these limited experiences led to very different conclusions about what the elephant must look like. Each blind man's description of the elephant sounded entirely contradictory to what the other two perceived. Had the three blind men resisted their argumentative tunnel vision by combining their descriptions rather than each insisting the elephant was a trunk, an ear, or a tail, they may have arrived at a more accurate picture of the elephant.

With what may appear to be contradictory statements God has wonderfully added dimension to his principles and purposes throughout the scriptures. Ah, but they are dimensional contributions to the same truth. It is fuller than a formula. It is truer than a phrase. It is not unlike Jesus' answer "I am the way, the truth, and the life".

Let me show you an example:

> He will turn the hearts of the fathers to their children, and the hearts of the children to their fathers; or else I will come and strike the land with a curse.
>
> **Malachi 4:6 (NIV)**

Nice; pleasant; reconciling.
This is the same God who also says through Jesus:

> For I have come to turn "a man against his father, a daughter against her mother, a daughter-in-law against her mother-in-law, a man's enemies will be the members of his own household."
>
> **Matthew 10:35-36 (NIV)**

Hard, unpleasant, and seemingly contradictory.

The question is this: Is God bringing unity or disunity to households? Has He come to bring peace or war?

I will answer this after we look at another example.

We all remember the fervent prayer of Jesus for unity in the Garden of Gethsemane written in John 17. In that prayer He used the word "sanctify" several times. Sanctify means to set apart. I think you can best understand what God wants to do by listening to His own words in part. I have added italics for emphasis.

> *Sanctify* them by the truth; your word is truth. As you sent me into the world, I have sent them into the world. For them I *sanctify* myself, that they too may be truly sanctified. My prayer is not for them alone. I pray also for those who will believe in me through their message, *that all of them may be one,* Father, just as you are in me and I am in you. May they also be in us so that the world may believe that you have sent me.I have given them the glory that you gave me, *that they may be one as we are one*: I in them and you in me. May they be brought to

> *complete unity* to let the world know that you sent me and have loved them even as you have loved me.
>
> **John 17:17-23 (NIV)**

Set apart—unite—separate—unify. Which is it? What is He asking?

Obviously, Jesus did not come to unite the world. If Jesus wanted to unite the world, surely He could have found something that everyone could have agreed on; something like, "Food for everyone", "Heaven for everyone", or "High self-esteem for everyone". Jesus wants us separated from lies, deception, and sin—but He wants us to be so united in love that He even aspires for us to be as united as He is with the Father!

And why does He want us to be separated from the world but united in holiness and truth? So the world will see and believe that it is God who sent Him and that God truly loves the world. The separation is not to form a clique or think ourselves better than the world, but to win the world.

Jesus came to separate His followers, God's people, from those who were in rebellion against God. He wants them to be set apart into the truth. Jesus' life is truth. It is crucial that we understand that unity which comes at the expense of truth is not godly unity. Unity without truth is a unity in lying. Unity in lies is just stupidity and falseness among the masses of humanity. Jesus raises an uncompromising standard. This standard of truth is the rallying point for holiness in God's redemptive love.

Jesus did not come to separate the church. He came to save it from deception. He came to purge it of its hypocrisy, dishonesty, half-heartedness, wickedness, and sinfulness—all sinfulness.

If God permitted un-holiness in His Church, it would not be an alternative to the world. It would not be relief from sin and death, but only some other form of sin and death. He must separate the wheat from the chaff. He must separate the sheep from the goats and He is the Judge who will decide what and who is to be saved or burned. It is our task to learn just what God requires.

The key point is this: If the love of Jesus separates, can our love be "better" than His? Impossible, if our love is different, it is inferior.

Let us ask, when is the truth not as important as family? This is a hard question.

According to Jesus, any relationship not based on truth isn't a worthwhile relationship. I am using deduction here. If truth sets free – lies bring bondage. Certainly, Jesus would never endorse a relationship that brings bondage. God loves us, but cannot have a relationship with us until our intentional offenses against love and truth are properly dealt with. Sin separates us from God and that is why God wants to separate us from sin.

This last sentence is so important I will write it again:

Sin separates us from God and that is why God wants to separate us from sin.

We must cling to the Word of God, even though it dramatically and drastically changes us. If you find things in the Bible that seem harsh or disagreeable to you, it is a good sign of two things: One, that you are honest and reading at face value. Second, you are not exactly like God. To see how you and God differ reveals your potential for growth. You are far ahead of those who seriously believe they agree with everything in the Bible intellectually and emotionally. We can claim it in faith, but there is still a big gap between our thoughts and God's. There is a huge chasm between our understanding and God's. Too many folks prefer to interpret scripture to fit into their current lifestyle; even we Christians. Many interpret the scripture to FIT into what they have decided is the right way to believe. This is self-deception and unfortunately, very common. We must not guard things simply because they are familiar to us. What we may call security, God may call bondage.

If we led the entire nation to the truth, there would be much greater unity than the constant lowering of standards for a broad common denominator produces.

If none are led to the truth but all to unity, there could be a great unity against God, similar to Babel.

If we lead some to the truth, there will be certain division and dissension.

If we led the entire nation to the truth and ALL served God, there would be a heavenly unity like this world has never seen.

What is your decision?

Remember this scripture quoted earlier by Jesus:

> I have come to bring fire on the earth, and how I wish it were already kindled! But I have a baptism to undergo, and how distressed I am until it is completed! Do you think I came to bring peace on earth? No, I tell you, but division. From now on there will be five in one family divided against each other, three against two and two against three. They will be divided, father against son and son against father, mother against daughter and daughter against mother, mother-in-law against daughter-in-law and daughter-in-law against mother-in-law.
>
> **Luke 12:49-53 (NIV)**

This doesn't sound like one big happy get together. If anything, Jesus seems to be the kind of person who causes trouble in families. To many, truth is trouble. Yet, Jesus is the model of love. He is three-dimensional truth.

Jesus values unity with God above unity among sinful men—and even family unity. Otherwise, He would not have said or prayed these things. Those who are sanctified in God's truth have the ultimate unity. They are united with each other, truth, and God Who is truth and love.

God is not looking to form exclusive clubs. ALL are invited. Actually, it is not God's Will that even one should perish.

Sin separates us from God and that is why God wants to separate us from sin. Italics added for emphasis.

> The Lord is not slow about His promise, as some count slowness, but is patient toward you, *not wishing for any to perish but for all to come to repentance.*
>
> **2 Peter 3:9 (NASB)**

LOVE HAS NO OPTION

Therefore, Jesus, as Son of our loving God, had no alternative. He was compelled by love to confront people with the truth regardless of the consequences. He was compelled by love to tell the people they can only find worthwhile unity in following God. They can never find satisfactory unity in following lies and the sinful ways of the world. They cannot find the complete unity of God's unity just by clinging to family relationships. We can never find satisfaction by seeking the lowest common denominator—something everyone will agree on. We can only find ultimate unity by holding fast to God's definitions of truth, His perfect law, His perfect love.

The hearts of the fathers will be turned to the children only when both father and children are seeking God's ways; only those who fear His Name and who purge themselves of wickedness. We must be able to tromp down wickedness. God will bring the most beautiful unity in families where all are seeking God's truth and love, however, those who seek the world's "truth and love" will be split away from those following God. This will bring division even in families.

Truth is not the bad guy. Sin is the bad guy.

Sin ruins relationships.

It is not truth, but lies that destroy genuine harmony.

ONLY THE DISCERNING CAN JUDGE

God is discussing restoration and says the following:

> And you will again see the distinction between the righteous and the wicked, between those who serve God and those who do not.
>
> **Malachi 3:18 (NIV)**

Throughout the book of Proverbs, Solomon makes a distinction between good and evil, righteous and unrighteousness, wisdom and foolishness. This discernment reveals wisdom, not hard-heartedness.

There is a rhythm to the back and forth comparison of "this is good and this is bad". You especially see this distinction made in chapters 10, 11, 12, 13, 14, and 15 of Proverbs to clarify the point. Let me give you examples selected just from Proverbs 10:

> A wise son makes a father glad, But a foolish son is a grief to his mother. Ill-gotten gains do not profit, But righteousness delivers from death.
>
> **Proverbs 10:1-2 (NASB)**

> Poor is he who works with a negligent hand, But the hand of the diligent makes rich. He who gathers in summer is a son who acts wisely, But he who sleeps in harvest is a son who acts shamefully. Blessings are on the head of the righteous, But the mouth of the wicked conceals violence.
>
> **Proverbs 10:4-6 (NASB)**

> He who walks in integrity walks securely, But he who perverts his ways will be found out.
>
> **Proverbs 10:9 (NASB)**

> Hatred stirs up strife, But love covers all transgressions.
>
> **Proverbs 10:12 (NASB)**

> Wise men store up knowledge, But with the mouth of the foolish, ruin is at hand.
>
> **Proverbs 10:14 (NASB)**

> The wages of the righteous is life, The income of the wicked, punishment. He is on the path of life who heeds instruction, But he who forsakes reproof goes astray.
>
> **Proverbs 10:16-17 (NASB)**

> When there are many words, transgression is unavoidable, But he who restrains his lips is wise.
>
> **Proverbs 10:19 (NASB)**

Doing wickedness is like sport to a fool; And so is wisdom to a man of understanding. What the wicked fears will come upon him, And the desire of the righteous will be granted.

Proverbs 10:23-24 (NASB)

The hope of the righteous is gladness, But the expectation of the wicked perishes. The way of the LORD is a stronghold to the upright, But ruin to the workers of iniquity. The righteous will never be shaken, But the wicked will not dwell in the land.

Proverbs 10:28-30 (NASB)

The lips of the righteous bring forth what is acceptable, But the mouth of the wicked, what is perverted.

Proverbs 10:32 (NASB)

See the back and forth comparisons to magnify the difference in practice and results?

In Leviticus, it is commanded to make a distinction between good and evil. It is not considered "being judgmental".

and so as to make a distinction between the holy and the profane, and between the unclean and the clean, and so as to teach the sons of Israel all the statutes which the LORD has spoken to them through Moses.

Leviticus 10:10-11 (NASB)

God has no problem communicating how severely He opposes the brutal abuse of His law by saying the priests have done "violence" to His law by NOT making a distinction between what is absolutely holy and absolutely profane.

Her priests have done violence to My law and have profaned My holy things; they have made no distinction between the holy and the profane, and they have not taught the difference between the unclean and the clean; and they hide their eyes from My sabbaths, and I am profaned among them.

Ezekiel 22:26-27 (NASB)

Many call this important quality "judgmental."

Discerning who is righteous and who is wicked is certainly not a character flaw but rather the ability from God necessary for obeying Him.

The real source of division between people and families is not truth, but rebellion or refusal to recognize and submit to the truth. This is why God wants us to separate from rebellion, not to bring disunity but greater unity.

A surgeon does not operate to wound or kill, but to heal or bring greater health.

God offers us the way to prosperity and peace in His unity, His truth, His love. Those who cannot follow these ways will eventually, if not from the start, be fighting one another. The unity based on lies is very flimsy. There is a difference between health and illness and so it is with morality and immorality. There is no love or wisdom in calling health and illness both good. Calling sickness "health" will not save the person from the symptoms and ultimate consequences of that illness.

Those who do stand for God's ways will be opposed by those who refuse to accept God's truth and love.

JESUS—WHY HIS LOVE CONFRONTS

If you watch Jesus in action, you can see Him constantly confronting people. He confronted selfishness, rebellion against God, demons, hypocrisy and unforgiveness at every turn. He would square off, face to face, against the wrongness of disloyalty to God.

Jesus is the essence of love confronting that which separates us from love. His confrontation is not to defeat people, but to redeem them. It is not to condemn, but to save. When they repented they were saved. When they refused to repent they felt offended by Jesus.

Jesus was not and is not a "positive thinker" when it comes to sin and unrighteousness. When He walked among us, He insisted on bringing into full focus the sinfulness of sin. Jesus was simply intolerant of sin—which is rebellion against God and the source of all grief to man. The fact that He did confront error proves the point. Confrontation can be great evidence of hope if it is done in a loving and wise manner. The hope reveals that truth DOES make a difference. The cutting pain of the truth is no more for injury than a wise surgeon's knife.

One rich, young man approached Jesus and asked how to be perfect ("complete" in some translations). This young man stated that he had kept all the commandments since his early youth. He wanted to know if he lacked anything. It is possible that such a devout and obedient man may have felt that only a positive response was forthcoming.

Sure, Jesus could have said something congratulatory or encouraging. After all, keeping the commandments since early youth is quite a feat for anyone at anytime in history. But the man had asked an honest question and deserved an honest answer. "Do I lack anything?"

This is how Jesus responded.

Jesus answered,

> "If you want to be perfect, go, sell your possessions and give to
> the poor, and you will have treasure in heaven.
> Then come, follow me."
>
> **Matthew 19:21 (NIV)**

Is Jesus fault finding or did He want to see the man completely set free and bearing fruit? This man had great potential and Jesus offered him the opportunity to fulfill that potential.

The rich young man walked away sad because he was unwilling to give up his riches. He asked Jesus. Jesus answered.

Jesus is much too loving to gloss over any sin. However, He is merciful enough to forgive any sin. Repentance is available and thanks to the wonderful mercy of God, forgiveness is available. We can even receive help from the Holy Spirit and the scriptures.

If a person is disturbed by reading his Bible because it indicates that his conduct or thinking is contrary, could that person find comfort and consolation in your church so he wouldn't have to repent? Do you understand my question? Are we helping or hindering the work of the Holy Spirit if the Spirit convicts a person of sin? Do we console the person in their sin or allow them to feel OK about that sin? How is making a person comfortable *in* their sin ever a Christian work? What good is it if we do that to ourselves?

The heart of our discussion in this chapter asks the question: Are we imitating Jesus when we avoid confronting sin or something "controversial"?

I have to show you something:

The world without God has only three (3) solutions for our wrongs, our sins.

1. Don't call it sin. *Call it normal* human behavior and keep saying it is OK; only condemn any who says that what you have done is wrong. "Everybody does it so don't feel bad."
2. *Justify it.* Don't say it's human, say it's admirable. Say under the circumstances it was absolutely the right thing to do. Change your morals to fit your conduct. Change your religious beliefs to fit your life so that what ever you have done is a "good thing".
3. *Deny it.* You never did it. You literally reprogram your memory to rewrite your history. Ultimately, you can believe your own lie to the point where you truly believe it more than reality.

It is surprising how easy it is to find many others who will agree, justify, and absolutely endorse things God plainly calls sin. They will even congratulate you, pat you on the back, and explain how good it is and that it is not wrong at all.

They also will condemn those that say your sin is wrong—including the Bible and God Himself. Or they may say certain scriptures no longer apply or they were inserted by men.

We personally make "merciful" excuses for friends and loved ones in regard to their sins because we care about them. I have done the same thing. Are we oracles of truth or of deception? In an attempt to protect them we may be insuring their personal destruction.

Do you feel God needs to be reproved and corrected for being so negative about sinfulness? Is God a pessimist? Is God just wrong? When we disagree with scripture, we are saying we are right and God is wrong.

Certainly a person like Jesus would be rejected by the majority of church people, just as we are today. Jesus flunks the course on "how to win friends and influence people" if we apply the world's standards. Instead of being charming, He was truthful and ruthless with sin because His love was so unerring.

Which doctor do you want? The one who destroys your disease or the one who makes you feel OK about having the disease?

When will the church at large realize that God has called us to proclaim truth in loving confrontation? The tolerating of sinfulness, lies, and error is a welcome mat for inevitable destruction in every arena of life.

Here are some lyrics to another one of my songs:

OH, THERE IS A GOD

What life has not suffered?
Whose eyes have not known tears?
Whose words have never been cruel?
To those that have loved us for years

What life has no shame?
Whose mind has no guilt?
Whose sleep has never been shortened
By a stab of regret in the night?

Oh, there is sin, but hope of forgiveness
Yes, there is pain, oh, rivers and rivers
But still there is God, His power can lift you
Oh, and his love, oceans and oceans for you

Your heart God knows
Your dreams God cherishes
And God dreams for you even greater dreams

Oh, there is sin, but hope of forgiveness
Yes, there is pain, oh, rivers and rivers
But still there is God, His power can lift you
Oh, and his love, oceans and oceans for you

CHAPTER THIRTEEN

✦ ✦ ✦

The Story of Daniel

Can you appreciate how easily I can get out of the Spirit and begin getting angry about my once godly nation consistently working to trivialize God, the Bible, Jesus Christ, and practically everything associated with Christianity?

It was not until later in life that the book of Daniel encouraged me like never before. This is an important chapter of this book if you allow it to sink in. I hope you do.

Permit me to give you the story of Daniel from my view.

Like most young men, Daniel must have had ambitious desires regarding the achievements in his life. Something devastating happened; the world as he knew it was destroyed and gone forever for the rest of his life. A foreign army came in and I am sure the nation of Judah put up a whole-hearted fight, but they were overcome by their enemies. There was bloodshed, casualties, fire, and destruction all around the young man Daniel and his fellow citizens. Many neighbors, friends, and family were killed and missing in the failed and valiant effort to defend their country and way of life. Now the leadership and government were gone. Now the invading foreigners began imposing their will on the nation with their new rules, new laws, and new government.

For Daniel, the change was even more severe. Besides being a young citizen of a now conquered people, he was to lose the surroundings of familiar faces, relatives, and his whole community. He was taken far away to the land of his captors—Babylon. His mother and father must have cried bitterly, if still alive.

Spiritually, Daniel was suddenly in a strange land of darkness. This was not just because it was a different culture and language. There were no religious hypocrites because there were no believers. The God of Israel, and Judah, was the foreign god of a foreign nation to the Babylonians and a "defeated" god at that.

Let me tell you why I am showing you the story of Daniel. Sadly, our generation has become dark and ungodly. Respected leaders of our land disobey God in many ways while invoking little criticism from citizens for being ungodly. Politicians can get in more trouble with voters by being openly obedient to God than disobedient. We have heroes, musicians and movie stars that are so popular even they stagger at the amount of money thrown at them. It is of no importance that they have no regard for God. They not only tolerate sin, often they model it, endorse it, flaunt it, and criticize anyone who dares to judge their lifestyle. Maybe they will thank God at awards ceremonies but what of the life they model for all. Many of our laws are similarly contrary to God even though our money says "In God We Trust".

Without the hypocrisy of a nation, Daniel lived in a land where his God was an unknown foreign god. This is far truer today in America than most believers realize. Surprisingly, Daniel lived in subjection to that land and its laws in a way that no Babylonians felt he was condescending to them, yet he still managed to remain totally loyal and obedient to God. Ponder this marvel.

Here is a model and example for us. Daniel remained steadfast in his commitment to obey God but he did not become brutishly defiant to the unbelievers. More importantly, Daniel did not lose heart.

Now I'll explain how the Babylonians did things. To assimilate conquered foreigners into Babylonian culture captives in training were given Babylonian names. Daniel was Jewish-Judean and they named him "Belteshazzar".

Daniel was selected as a Jewish "prize" to be taught Babylonian ways. This was to increase not only his potential, but to spread Babylonian culture, religion, and their way of thinking as a model to the Jews. This assimilation of various representatives from around the world was also a good public relations display of the world being a better place under Babylonian domination; a notably intelligent strategy for turning notions of rebellion held by conquered people toward possibly gaining ambitions of succeeding peacefully in this "improved" society. Such was the stuff for maintaining unity and peace in a conquered world. Young men like Daniel were schooled and trained to read and write in the Babylonian culture. They were taught history from the Babylonian perspective. They were trained in Babylonian etiquette. They were not treated as downtrodden slaves but rather valuable specimens imported from conquered lands to be refined in Babylonian ways.

Believers in every single generation must choose between the norms of his culture and the kingdom of God. It is no different for you and me right now. What was normal in the 1950's is far from normal today. Still there was sin then and plenty of it. But if we tried to take today's accepted forms of entertainment and behavior to the 1940's or 1950's we would be considered deviant, immoral people unfit for American society. But God is not trying to take us back to the 1940's or 1950's as nostalgic as it may seem to us. God is calling us to holiness, love, and freedom from sin and fear.

Jesus Christ is the same yesterday and today, yes and forever.

Hebrews 13:7-9 (NASB)

I hear many folks today complain they have difficulty growing spiritually because of their "dead" church. They do not realize they accuse God of being unable to reach willing hearts.

Daniel did not attend a great church. He didn't have Christian TV. He had no real godly accountability except possibly a pact with his friends. Nearly every influence in his life was anti-God or unaware of God. Ungodliness was the overwhelming influence in Daniel's life. As he assimilated into the Babylonian culture he, by his own choice, did not stray from our God. Instead Daniel grew in faithfulness to God, in God's wisdom, and His principles.

There is a saying, "Friends are like phosphorous, seen plainest when all around is dark." Are we God's friends?

When all around us is dark and all positive peer pressure and accountability seems to vanish, then we discover the intent of our heart. Nothing could impair Daniel's growth in God because this was an uncompromising choice he made. Actually, because of his circumstances and fixed resolve to serve God, his growth was most likely *accelerated* by the constant ungodly challenges to his faith. It is resistance that strengthens our muscles, not relaxation.

To me, here is some very exciting news. Daniel's life of obedience to God was far brighter because of the overwhelming darkness.

A flashlight in daylight seems dim. However at night, a flashlight can be seen from a great distance. A white rose among many red roses stands out as most beautiful, yet a red rose among many white roses would stand out as more distinct and beautiful. In the same way, righteousness among the self-indulgent has the distinction by contrast. It is natural. The exception is always more noticeable. One Bible-believer among many unbelievers has the privilege and the burden of literally defining for all those unbelievers what faith in Christ is all about. Do you blend in? Do you excuse your sin because you are so outnumbered? Remember, if it is known you are a believer, it is because you are outnumbered that you have the spotlight. It is because you are so outnumbered that you truly have a tremendous opportunity to witness without words. People interpret what you do.

Being different is always noticeable. We need to be noticed but admirable, not noticed as weird or hypocritical. Certainly no one will admire us when they notice us and we are looking down our noses at them either.

OBSERVATION: Notice that the government was not one where the people governed. Daniel did not have a voice as a citizen. Daniel did not have legal rights. In this capacity he served God and others. He served others who had their own god. Daniel gained such respect and notoriety for the excellence of his work and character he was promoted again and again. Eventually Daniel was given a voice, given authority, given the ability to influence not only others, but even influence the supreme leader himself, Nebuchadnezzar.

While many others tried to make "evil" of the Jewish God and the worship of the true God a crime, Daniel lived an exemplary life drawing attention to integrity, wisdom, and the power of his God. Because of Daniel's life, God was honored, even by Nebuchadnezzar; this in an ungodly realm. The other gods took a back seat to Daniel's God because of Daniel.

> The king answered Daniel and said, "Surely your God is a God of gods and a Lord of kings and a revealer of mysteries, since you have been able to reveal this mystery." Then the king promoted Daniel and gave him many great gifts, and he made him ruler over the whole province of Babylon and chief prefect over all the wise men of Babylon.
>
> **Daniel 2:47-49 (NASB)**

Do our lives, without a word, bring honor to God? God has never called His people to boast of their true God in a condescending manner. God never told us to look down on others or proclaim to others they are going to hell.

> Or do you think lightly of the riches of His kindness and forbearance and patience, not knowing that the kindness of God leads you to repentance?
>
> **Romans 2:4 (NASB)**

There is no way we can picture Daniel telling everybody how bad they are and how good he is because he believes in the right God and they believe in false gods. He didn't elevate himself above others, he served them with excellence and it drew attention.

In fact, scripture teaches that God favors humility.

> And before honor comes humility.
>
> **Proverbs 15:33 (NASB)**

Before destruction the heart of man is haughty, But humility goes before honor.

Proverbs 18:12 (NASB)

Seek the LORD, All you humble of the earth Who have carried out His ordinances; Seek righteousness, seek humility. Perhaps you will be hidden In the day of the LORD'S anger.

Zephaniah 2:3 (NASB)

If the Bible is God's Word, then God declares that anyone who says he loves God but does not love other people is a flat out liar.

If someone says, "I love God," and hates his brother, he is a liar; for the one who does not love his brother whom he has seen, cannot love God whom he has not seen.

1 John 4:20 (NASB)

Who in the world does God *not* love? No one; God loves all. Who in the world are we permitted to not love? No one; we are to love all. Are we then to approve of all lifestyles and philosophies? Of course not! To accept all sins and all gods is nothing but accepting all error.

Daniel exemplifies for us the kind of life we should and can lead. We should not complain about the ungodliness around us or the lack of action other believers are taking. Instead, we should be critical about *our own* hypocrisy. We should and can allow God to convict us of our own sins and be the brightest light we can, obeying God, pleasing God, serving Him diligently. We should call out to God and pray for our nation, other believers and those around us.

Daniel seemed to love the ungodly kings he served. He was no flatterer. He loved God even more than he loved any king, government, or position. Without a single word, Daniel's actions proved this. He risked his life more than once because of his devotion to God.

Does our life reflect God's holiness?

Does our life reveal God's values?

Does our life prove our love for God and those we serve?

Are we examples of wisdom or foolishness; of integrity or hypocrisy?

Do we talk a lot to distract listeners from noticing our compromising and contradictory lifestyles? Do we try to gloss over our life with our words?

Is our manner of living preaching the same message we want others to believe when we do speak?

This is very basic Christianity. Abandon dishonesty. Abandon hypocrisy.

Way back in 1973, after graduating from Youth With A Mission in 1972, and doing a music tour, I felt I should go back to my father's house in New Jersey. I had previously run away from home in 1970 when barely 17 and now I was 19, saved, and sanctified. I was going to be a witness to my father and step-mother. I thought I was a big star having talked at churches all over the east coast area and in Jamaica. They didn't see it that way.

My dad sat me down and even though he was not a believer at that time, told me not to try to preach to everyone but just say whatever I had to say without words. Being good at spontaneity, I naturally responded that of course that was my intention. I suddenly realized beyond any doubt that my life and my preaching were totally different and I needed to repent fast enough for my dad to not notice my hypocrisy. It was one of the best things that ever happened to me.

If you know these things, you are blessed *if you do them.*

John 13:17 (NASB)

(Italics added by the author)

Although the life of Daniel, as all righteous men, brought light where many would prefer darkness, he thrived. Although the life of Daniel did not show approval of sin, many sinners approved of Daniel.

By the way, Daniel's Chaldean name, "Belteshazzar", means "who lays up treasures in secret".

Even secular movies celebrate love, honesty, loyalty, courage, wisdom, and integrity.

The character of Jesus, as exemplified by Daniel, is the core Christian integrity we need before we even begin criticizing sinfulness aloud in others. Daniel is a terrific example of how Americans who follow Christ need to put Christ ABOVE politics but not INSTEAD of community leadership. In a world without God's light, we need the faithful to step up and lead. Daniel was a significant part of an ungodly government without sinning against God.

Jesus was not famous for attacking sinners, but for attacking religious hypocrisy. Hmmm, who would Jesus verbally attack today?

If Daniel lived in America, he would be well respected. But if given the right, the privilege, the duty of "governing" as a citizen in a government of, by and for the people, we would see, I believe, a more verbal, outspoken saint.

We have different callings and talents. The only commands I am sure we all have in common is to love at all times, to speak the truth and not lie, and to always obey God.

I hope these lessons from his life are now secret treasures uncovered for you.

CHAPTER FOURTEEN

✦ ✦ ✦

Love in Action

LOVE AT WAR

ince sin has existed, God has been at war. He will continue to be until sin is abolished. God is much too loving to do otherwise.

> The Lord is a man of war.
>
> **Exodus 15:3 (KJV)**

God is not negotiating for an arrangement where light and darkness can agree, but is out to conquer, overcome, and reign. Therefore, His people should not be seeking peaceful relations with ungodliness, in themselves or anyone else.

Holiness does not tolerate sin. Once it does, it is no longer holy. Righteousness wars with sin. If it doesn't, it is not true righteousness. Love forgives, but once it compromises it becomes adulterated.

Michael the Archangel never did respect Lucifer's self made doctrine.

Jesus never made deals with demons.

Moses never compromised with the Pharaoh.

Elijah did not seek a truce with the prophets of Baal.

> Elijah said unto them "Take the prophets of Baal; let not one of them escape" And they took them: and Elijah brought them down to the brook Kishon, and slew them there.
>
> **1 Kings 18:40 (KJV)**

Elijah seems to show little sympathy toward his fellow man. Why? Hating sin IS loving the sinner. They were leading Israel astray, sacrificing children, and would gladly kill Elijah.

First, all followers of God are against sin, not the sinner. Our hearts should be full of mercy while having just and righteous actions. To be uncompromising against sin is to be truly sympathetic toward man. As stated previously, "Do you want a doctor who respects all life, including influenza and cancer cells that are hurting you?"

Secondly, anyone who stands for anything always has enemies. In this particular instance, the Israelites were ready to kill either Elijah or the prophets of Baal. This was obvious even before the contest began. The people knew that the two could not co-exist. The beliefs were directly opposed. God proved Himself, and then Elijah instructed the people. It was the logical and understood conclusion of this conflict. There was the victor and the defeated. God wins, Baal loses. The true prophet lives, the false prophets die. Elijah instructed the people accordingly.

Jesus said:

> He that is not with me is against me; and he that gathereth not with me scattereth abroad.
>
> **Matthew 12:30 (KJV)**

God will not award approval to those of us who sacrifice the truth for comfort among our peers. God is always against the destructiveness of lies and corruption destroying people. If you are compatible with sin, you are incompatible with God. If that is what any of us do, it is not God that we are loyal to, but our own contrary cause.

Any cause of "self-preservation" at the expense of our generation, our families, and the truth is to turn against God, as politically incorrect as that may sound.

God's people are called to warfare. Paul said:

> Finally, be strong in the Lord, and in the strength of His might. Put on the full armor of God, that you may be able to stand firm against the schemes of the devil. For our struggle is not against flesh and blood, but against the rulers, against the powers, against the world forces of this darkness, against the spiritual forces of wickedness in the heavenly places.
>
> **Ephesians 6:10-12 (NASB)**

Most of us shrink back from being openly against anything.

Did you observe the distinction Paul made between the rulers, powers, and *world forces* of darkness? Then he specified the *spiritual forces* of wickedness.

There are TWO different powers we struggle against; worldly and spiritual forces, but *neither* is flesh. Our war is with world forces and spiritual forces. Look carefully at that scripture again.

Until all sin is abolished, godly love is at war because sin destroys people.

BEHIND ENEMY LINES—AN OPPORTUNITY

Recognize that to be on God's side in this world is to automatically be behind enemy lines. Just because of a decision in my heart, opposition now surrounds me. What was once home is now my war zone. I am now calling a place I've never seen, except by faith, my homeland.

However, since I am indeed behind the enemy lines, I can sabotage, recruit converts, give vital information, and expect tremendous support from my allies in heaven and earth as I work for our victory.

To win battles I must be willing to suffer wounds while my new homeland will no doubt provide ammunition, food, direction, and all the tools I need in my daring attempts to thwart my enemies' plans.

If I was in my homeland far from these front lines, I could only hear about the battle, but while I am alive in this sinful world, my Lord will put me in contact with other agents of our kingdom. I go, entrusting myself to this cause. I know I can do more for my homeland where I am now, behind enemy lines, than anywhere else.

TO QUALIFY VICTORY

God is at war in this battle against sin. If you are not with Him, He says you are against Him.

If you have no enemies, you have no battle and you will have no victory.

You cannot have victory without a battle.

You cannot have a battle unless you have a specific enemy.

To qualify a victory, one needs not only to have an enemy, but must also defeat that enemy. This is exactly God's intention, to defeat the enemy.

Jesus' work is not finished until all of His enemies are totally defeated.

> . . . After that comes the end [the completion], when He delivers over the kingdom to God the Father after rendering inoperative and abolishing every [other] rule and every authority and power. For [Christ] must be king and reign until He has put all [His] enemies under His feet. The last enemy to be subdued and abolished is death.
>
> **1 Corinthians 15:24-26 (AMP)**

The Bible is seasoned with words like, "overcoming" and "conquering". Listen to the declaration in such scriptural communication. It frequently visits battles and wars in the Old Testament, while the New Testament talks of spiritual battle and warfare.

> . . . we are more than conquerors through him who loved us.
>
> **Romans 8:37 (NIV)**

. . . for everyone born of God overcomes the world. This is the victory that has overcome the world, even our faith.

1 John 5:4 (NIV)

I saw heaven standing open and there before me was a white horse, whose rider is called Faithful and True. With justice he judges and makes war.

Revelation 19:11 (NIV)

The God of peace will soon crush Satan under your feet.

Romans 8:20 (NIV)

It was never intended for Christians to huddle around and defend some cliquish refuge. No, they are CONQUERORS OUT CONQUERING! They are on the offense not the defense, hunting and purging out the evil, leaving no rock unturned. Even Satan's last defense will be found and destroyed. The defensive home gates of hell cannot withstand the zeal of God's righteousness through His people. Wickedness is to be COMPLETELY defeated.

In light of these goals, how could we realistically expect our enemies to tolerate us, let alone pay us compliments?

Of course, we will be tagged "radical", "domineering", "oppressive", "extreme", "strange", "judgmental", "extremists", "fanatics", "ignorant", and a horde of other names. Should we back off?

We shouldn't even flinch. In our run for being faithful, there is one vote we want—God's.

Above all, we are called to love, not to condemn. This is where thousands of zealous church folk and even terrorists have totally missed it.

We are certainly no better than anyone else. It is true that obeying God is right and disobeying him is foolish. Part of that obedience is condemning sin, but never, never condemning the people God wants to save from sin. Who does God want to save from sin? The answer is ALL. Much of our modern day terrorism is the result of a great devotion to a particular religion or the idea of hating people of a different faith. Self-righteousness in any faith or denomination is a conceit considering non-members as inferior or disposable. This was also the Pharisees perception of others. Since God loves all people, we will find ourselves most like God when we love all people.

What we really have as believers, in the Word of God and from Jesus Christ, could be likened to a cure for cancer or AIDS. What is humble or loving about agreeing with others that there is no cure? Or for that matter, respecting all religions is like pretending there are many cures if we know there is only one that actually works. To allow dying people to be treated with cures we know don't work and remain silent about the real cure would indeed be cruel. And it is ridiculous to portray "loving" in a way that denies the reality of Jesus Christ, God's truth, and what His mercy can do for all of us.

The earth didn't invent itself. The marvelous order of all of nature is not the result of chaotic random accidents. He created us and all that exists. He came and is coming again.

God's Will, His blessing, and His truth as displayed from Genesis to Revelation by His Holy Spirit, is that which sets free; not as a religion but as the reality of God Himself!

Anything contrary to God's values is lofty speculation that deceives and destroys. It is our enemy and God's. This is practical. Who is comfortable with the idea of being told lies? If I believe something that is erroneous, wrong, or a lie—I truly want to know about it. I want to know what is really true, don't you?

Now here is a politically incorrect announcement:

> *GOD* has the right to destroy His enemies.

Our faith in Christ is far more than escaping hell. It is bent on conquest. Hell and death are not just prisons, but real enemies that will actually be defeated by God's obedient servants through Jesus Christ!

Hell and sin cannot tolerate true Christianity and true Christianity cannot tolerate hell and sin. These are forever incompatible. Only one can prevail.

I ask you, since there is reward for the just and faithful, punishment for the unjust and unfaithful, and no third place for those who insist on being neither . . . where shall God send those who insist they are neither for nor against sin?

CHAPTER FIFTEEN

✦ ✦ ✦

Volunteer Mission or Sin of Omission

"Those people who will not be governed by God
will be ruled by tyrants."

William Penn

The Christian church in America does not have the reputation of protecting the community and its citizens, and it's too bad. It appears to most non-church members that the church is only protecting itself.

Is the church known for standing up for the rights of the downtrodden? The ACLU claims to be. Is the church in America bigger than the ACLU? Yes, it is enormously larger but acts much weaker. Churches are famous for caring mostly about themselves or their own denomination. Are churches even known for protecting the other churches of a different denomination in the same community? Rarely!

This, dear reader, is not a reputation of love, but rather some kind of exclusive club recruiting paying members.

No wonder the unsaved so often reject the church. We are strife-torn, divided, bickering among denominations, and too often, even within one congregation.

This must change.

SELF-IMPOSED SILENCE

There are people in other lands that are literally dying for speaking out against evil in their lands. They are being silenced by oppressive governments or militia. Not us, we are silent because we don't want to appear impolite, judgmental, or politically off-center, so we silence ourselves and the abominations multiply exponentially with our consent.

Oh, you disagree?

We have the right to vote, the right to speak, the right to publish, the right to protest, the right to run for office, the right to work in every arena of public service, and be disagreeable to the onslaught of ungodly laws and practices.

We mostly prefer to discuss these things in private among ourselves.

Too many Christians are hiding behind their Bibles.

Obviously, there are a huge number of people who believe in love, God, mercy, and justice but do not practice God's commandments if it means expense, inconvenience, sacrifice—or confrontation.

LOVE HATES HOW SIN RUINS PEOPLE

Again, because of the many horrible errors in history committed by those claiming to represent God, let me echo God's Word in the next few sentences. Confrontation alone does not mean that we are obedient. Condemning sinners does not make us obedient. Pretending to be better than others does not make us obedient. LOVE, real LOVE, nothing but God's LOVE filling us is what makes us righteously intolerable toward that which destroys the adults and children that live all around us.

> Now the deeds of the flesh are evident, which are: immorality, impurity, sensuality, idolatry, sorcery, enmities, strife, jealousy, outbursts of anger, disputes, dissensions, factions, envying, drunkenness, carousing, and things like these, of which I forewarn you just as I have forewarned you that those who practice such things shall not inherit the kingdom of God.

> But the fruit of the Spirit is love, joy, peace, patience, kindness, goodness, faithfulness, gentleness, self-control; against such things there is no law. Now those who belong to Christ Jesus have crucified the flesh with its passions and desires. If we live by the Spirit, let us also walk by the Spirit. Let us not become boastful, challenging one another, envying one another.
>
> **Galatians 5:19-26 (NASB)**

How great it would be if we had the fruits of the Spirit in dealing with one another at work, at home, within our church, with other churches, and with the world. Apparently, love, joy, peace, patience, kindness, goodness, faithfulness, gentleness, and self-control are characteristics that God wills for His servants.

I often refrain from discussing abortion openly because abortion is so common. My opinion offends folks and sometimes it hurts their feelings. I must say that it is not unusual for folks to completely agree also. But the heart of God is not for those with the same opinion to find each other and talk about others. God wants us all to love one another, pray for each other, and seek out restoration and healing for all that are willing.

Abortion does not just kill innocent children, it devastates mothers. We are not interested in just saving the children, but saving the parents as well.

God does not want to destroy homosexuals. Yes, He did it in Sodom and Gomorrah, but He loves them as much as He loves you or Jesus Christ. Do not ever doubt this. This is great love that God has, so be careful. They say God approves all love. It is true, He does. But brotherly love has nothing to do with sex. That is what God condemns. God approves all love. God does not approve all sex. That is not my opinion, but pure Bible. God wants to save homosexuals from their sin as much as He wants to save adulterers and fornicators from their equally awful sin. God wants to save liars and religious hypocrites from their equally awful sin also. God condemns all sin. God loves all people. Sin destroys people. God loves people. Sin's destructive nature cannot be changed by people saying it isn't so bad.

You may feel like the whole world disagrees with you just for agreeing with God sometimes. The whole world can't be wrong and you right can it? Ask Noah.

Suffering is not God's punishment but usually the horrible consequences of stupidity that God continually seeks to save us from. Sin separates us all from happiness, the very pleasure God desires for us to enjoy in abundance. The truly humble and faithful loves sinners without abandoning the perfect wisdom of His Word. The Bible is very clear on this. These are dramatic issues. Just as important are the issues of our lack of love and our self-righteousness.

AVOID OR INCUR GOD'S WRATH

As we already discussed in Leviticus, God declared that He would set Himself against the man and his family who neglected to punish, by death, anyone who gave his offspring to Molech. Giving your child to Molech was sacrificing the life of your child to an idol.

Even if you think I am stretching it when I call current "pursuit of happiness" a cultic mentality, consider how that inspiring phrase has been reshaped to license anything that pleases us, including the "sacrifice" of unwanted children—you cannot deny what God says in Leviticus. It clearly calls the people who don't speak out against this sin as "harlots after the same sin". In God's eyes silence is not only consent, but that consenting silence and omission in stopping the crime is considered being an accessory to the crime.

> If the people of the community close their eyes when that man gives one of his children to Molech and they fail to put him to death, I will set my face against that man and his family and will cut off from their people both him and all who follow him in prostituting themselves to Molech.
>
> **Leviticus 20:4-5**

God was so angry because they did not stop or punish this awful crime that in His wrath He vowed to punish those believers; not for offering sacrifices to Molech, but for not punishing those who did. I am not reading into this. Read it again yourself.

God not only is saying that silence is consent but uses stronger words. He says they are prostituting themselves to the same false god.

How could any loving people in any society or period in history ignore the murder of innocent children?

How could a loving people in America remain silent? Not just once. Not just twice. Not just a hundred times, but more than thousands, *more than all the American casualties of all the American wars put together*—millions. If we ever condemn church-going Germans for not at least protesting the murder of millions of Jews, remember that the ghastly casualties were far less than those of our own children. In America this is not committed by some insane tyrant who hates an ethnic group, but a law telling mothers they can sacrifice their children on the altar of the pursuit of their own happiness, and the "priests" that kill the child are paid. In America it is all legal and we "educate" mothers internationally to do the same. We like to call it "a woman controlling her own body". *Birth control is a woman controlling her body; abortion is stopping another body from continuing to live.* The carnage continues full steam as you read these words. It is a profitable billion dollar industry. I could go on about how millions of those dollars could be rerouted to help people with real medical needs instead of killing future taxpayers.

Future history will remember our culture in a manner similar to other cultures that practiced human sacrifice. It is grotesque.

Obviously, because of the sheer numbers, I know many reading this have had an abortion or are close to someone who did. I think this may be true for most of us, if not all of us. Many regret it. I only hope we can change the legality of it so good people like you help others stay away from it. If abortion was illegal, millions of good law-abiding folks would not consider it. Even if they didn't like the law, millions of lives would be saved. Just being alive and unwanted is not a crime worthy of execution.

If, dear reader, you stop reading and want to weep, please bookmark the page and come back. I don't know how we can refrain from weeping.

I will state right now that if you don't run for office, if you don't protest publicly, if you don't volunteer for community service, if you don't write letters to congressmen, politicians, or the newspaper—please, at least pray and vote. It may well be all God wants you to do.

If a mere 5% more Christians voted, it would change the direction of the nation, just 5%! Where are the Christians?

God wants us to submit to Him, not to the world.

God wants us to obey His Word, not our own slant on things.

God wants us to be correct, not be politically correct.

God wants us to change from glory to glory. He doesn't want us to change His Word from chapter to chapter.

Will we repent or shall we "humbly" accept exile?

> Woe to you who are complacent in Zion, and to you who feel secure on Mount Samaria, you notable men of the foremost nation, to whom the people of Israel come! Therefore you will be among the first to go into exile; your feasting and lounging will end.
>
> **Amos 6:1, 7 (NIV)**

If we refuse to vote—if we refuse to run for office—we are telling pagans and atheists to rule and govern us. We are accelerating our own destruction and exile. Our silence is consent to all the evils in our generation. God will not help us if we make no effort to obey Him in these areas. In truth, in addition to the consequences of our turning over the nation to ungodliness we also incur God's wrath for our refusal to help or take a stand.

Knowing God, He probably has already commissioned many Christians to run for office on local, county, state, and national levels.

Knowing Satan, he probably suggested to many of these same Christians that it was not God's call but rather a pompous thought motivated by ego. Too many of these commissioned people have turned back to other pursuits in an attempt to be a "humble and lowly Christian". I have gone through this many times myself; even in regard to publishing this book I asked, "Who am I?" I am just another sinner who has seen the painful error of my own ways and know I might help others.

VOLUNTEER!

Somebody has to help. Somebody has to start. Somebody has to care. Somebody has to obey.

Are you going to wait for some movement to join? Are you waiting for a better movement that you feel you can trust? Are you waiting for your church to do something? Are you ready to privately respond to God's Holy Spirit right now?

In the book of Judges Deborah and Barak were grateful for God's blessing on the VOLUNTEERS. Volunteers are people with initiative.

> That the leaders led in Israel, that the people volunteered, bless the LORD!
>
> **Judges 5:2 (NASB)**

The same verse in another translation says,

> When the princes in Israel take the lead, when the people willingly offer themselves—praise the LORD!
>
> **Judges 5:2 (NIV)**

These volunteers risked their lives to throw off oppression.

Christians in America can again be inspiring people of courage and love.

Obedience to God is never to be delayed until others obey. This will get none of us off the hook with God.

VOTE!

We have already *given* most of the responsibility of feeding the hungry, teaching our children, writing and enforcing law, and governing our nation, primarily to those who do not serve God. How? By not voting, not running, not helping, not campaigning, not volunteering, not speaking a word or voicing even an opinion among those that may disagree. Silence is consent.

If the Christians do not lead this nation in righteousness, who will? If we let atheists and the enemies of God lead our nation, where will they lead us?

We choose our leaders by voting or by not voting. We can get ourselves into leadership--in church, community, and country or not get into leadership.

Getting into leadership and leading righteously is not worldly ambition. As godly leaders we are battling sin as ambassadors of Christ in a lost world.

Politics is the art of leadership. Dare we, the only ones with the knowledge of God's truth, force this leadership onto atheists? Who do you want to run your country, state, county, city, and your school boards? Do you want non-theists, enemies of God, pagans, or folks that keep saying they believe one thing but do another? We cannot change these things by a steadfast resolve of un-involvement. This cannot make sense.

Our current situation is more like this—voting is a privilege to some and to others a right. However, to hundreds of thousands of Christians it is an inconvenience.

The right to vote ... our form of government ... has been provided for us at the expense of many lives in American history. Truthfully, even though no one hears about it in history classes or textbooks, it has been mostly Christian lives. Not exclusively Christian and not with entirely pure motives, but easily far more than 50% of all Americans that died in wars from the Revolutionary War, the Civil War [both sides], World War I and World War II have been Christian believers. The disregard of God in America is a new thing. For most of American history to be American was practically by default, to be a Christian. The rebellion of students in the 1940's was chewing gum and talking in class. It is not the nation it once was.

Today, it is confirmed through polls, that we have a more moral America than actual voting reflects. Why is this? It is because 20-30%

of the morally upright citizens *don't vote* or even register to vote.

For example, polls typically show about 85% of the public is against pornography. Only 65% will make the trip to the polls to make that opinion count.

If just 25% of these non-voting moral people would vote, 90% of the elections could very well be changed. The reason for this drastic effect is because frequently only 5% of the vote is the determining factor in an election.

I repeat politics is the art of leadership. Dare we, the only ones with knowledge of God's truth, force this leadership onto atheists and enemies of God by our refusal to get involved?

IF YOU OBEY, OTHERS WILL FOLLOW

"Silence is consent." Silent believers are all around us. We are all waiting for someone to do something true, right, and courageous. We'd vote for someone like that. We would agree with someone like that.

We must take that lead, carefully, lovingly, with wisdom. Stop waiting. Listen to God.

How is the church supposed to change this country for the glory of God, by earnestly praying for atheists to speak and act with Christian values?

Shall we continue to pray for the trend to turn by *not* voting and then praying that the other citizens in America will vote correctly?

Since we Christian Americans have been given much liberty and much more responsibility in maintaining righteousness in our nation than most citizens in the world, the words of Jesus aptly apply to us:

> But the one who does not know and does things deserving punishment will be beaten with few blows. From everyone who has been given much, much will be demanded; and from the one who has been entrusted with much, much more will be asked.
>
> **Luke 12:48 (NIV)**

In America, God's children may be on the hot seat with God more than anywhere else because we have Bibles, we go to church, and we hear the truth.

Citizens are part of the governing body in America. As part of the governing body in America we have the opportunity and duty to protect the innocent and to proclaim wisdom, values, righteousness, and honor for our Lord and those in our country. Our nation could become a testimony to the world of God's wisdom, as it once was here and as it once was with Solomon.

> King Solomon was greater in riches and wisdom than all the other kings of the earth. The whole world sought audience with Solomon to hear the wisdom God had put in his heart.
>
> **1 Kings 10:23-24** (NIV)

What a splendid testimony! All the kings of the earth sought this man who was serving God to hear the wisdom that God had given him.

Where are God's ambassadors earning such praises? What is our attractiveness to the world? Is it our service, our wisdom, our kindness, our leadership, or just our wealth?

There are churches everywhere. The yellow pages are filled with churches. Where is the impact on our communities with so many churches?

I am not ignoring the true heroes; I am speaking to the masses. The heroes are called heroes because they are the exception.

What kind of example are we to our young if we wash our hands of involvement with respect to the law, government, our citizenship, freedom of the press, or freedom of speech? There are so many open doors that still beckon men of wisdom and character to speak out? Your country needs you.

This book was originally written in 1979 and distributed on a small scale. More than 20 years has passed and I had to change the tense on so many paragraphs warning about how things could get bad in America. I have had to change things to "too late" because we have crossed that threshold. Repentance did not occur. The reign of ungodliness has permeated so deeply that many Christian practices are now illegal. Twenty years ago I spoke of it coming; now it is behind us. Twenty years ago this book was more of a call to a *defensive* rally; now all that is left is an uprising against much greater and more established ungodly strongholds at every level of government, school, in textbooks, educational programs, and entertainment. I could write an entire book just itemizing the decline of our nation during the past 20 years but it would only depress us.

In the 1950's, a young rebel looked authority in the face and did wrong. James Dean starred in "Rebel without a Cause". He defied the standards of his time.

Today, a young rebel would defy our standards by being a virgin by choice and having no need of condoms. The rebel would insist on praying to Jesus or God in public, ignoring the crowd's disapproval. The rebel would bring a Bible to school saying evolution is still a theory, and an unscientific one at that, ridiculing the science textbooks and the teacher. Rebels would say homosexuality is wrong and unnatural, causing listeners jaws to drop. These defiant types would reject the euphemism "fling" and insist on using the term "adultery" and call "fooling around" "fornication". They themselves would be called "troublemakers", and "disrespectful". Folks would shake their heads as these "troublemakers" insist on honoring and obeying their parents even if the teacher keeps saying their parents are wrong. They would be sent to the principal's office for calling abortion "murder". In today's school environment, who knows, maybe a social worker would be called to evaluate the misconduct of the parents.

We still have plenty of potential but we have a fight on our hands; first, in the local community.

SILENCE IS CONSENT—If we allow an evil to continue in our community, are we not teaching our children to conclude that a particular evil is OK because the community approves? Mom and Dad may object verbally to the evil at the dinner table, but the children know that the WHOLE community approves; the child can assume Mom and Dad must be wrong. How can you convince them you are not wrong? It will certainly not be by silence or mere dinner table criticism.

CITIZEN STEWARDSHIP

Look at this story Jesus told:

> Again, it will be like a man going on a journey, who called his servants and entrusted his property to them. To one he gave five talents of money, to another two talents, and to another one talent, each according to his ability. Then he went on his journey. The man who had received the five talents went at once and put his money to work and gained five more. So also, the one with the two talents gained two more. But the man who had received the one talent went off, dug a hole in the ground and hid his master's money. After a long time the master of those servants returned and settled accounts with them. The man who had received the five talents brought the other five. "Master," he said, "you entrusted me with five talents. See, I have gained five more."
>
> His master replied, "Well done, good and faithful servant! You have been faithful with a few things; I will put you in charge of many things. Come and share your master's happiness!" The man with the two talents also came. "Master," he said, "you entrusted me with two talents; see, I have gained two more." His master replied, "Well done, good and faithful servant! You have been faithful with a few things; I will put you in charge of many things. Come and share your master's happiness!" Then the man who had received the one talent came. "Master," he said, "I knew that you are a hard man, harvesting where you have not sown and gathering where you have not scattered seed. So I was afraid and went out and hid your talent in the ground. See, here is what belongs to you." His master replied, "You wicked, lazy servant! So you knew that I harvest where I have not sown and gather where I have not scattered seed? Well then, you should have put my money on deposit with the bankers, so that when I returned I would have received it back with interest. Take the talent from him and give it to the one who has the ten talents. For everyone who has will be given more, and he will have an abundance. Whoever does not

have, even what he has will be taken from him. And throw that worthless servant outside, into the darkness, where there will be weeping and gnashing of teeth."

Matthew 25:14-30 (NIV)

Here is a character that did nothing against His master other than not take advantage of the opportunity which his master provided. Just for that, his master called him "wicked", "lazy", and "worthless". His master punished him as well.

If we could measure liberty and peace by talents, haven't we received many talents of gold from our forefathers and God? Are we investing that liberty and peace so there is more or less liberty and peace for our grandchildren? Are we investing that golden freedom that so many have defended and died for? Many died nobly so we could live nobly.

If these privileges were the talents in this parable, would the Master give us more or take what He gave us away?

Even as late as the hour is in America—we can still repent. Judgment is upon us. Really, it is here now. Real Christianity has already been defeated in America. Christianity is a big religion in America but it is no longer the strength of America; I believe it still can be.

Here are lyrics to another one of my songs.

AMERICA ONCE LOVED THE LORD

THIS LAND OF MINE it was blessed by the Lord
Established by men so determined and sure
Their blood on this land, their stand was "truth should live free"

America once loved the Lord
America loves Him no more
TURN BACK TO GOD

The rivers flowed. No taxes on homes
Each carried his load and cared for his own
Children surrounded by loved ones and old ones were never alone

America once loved the Lord
America loves Him no more

TURN BACK TO GOD, TURN BACK TO GOD

THIS LAND OF MINE it was blessed by the Lord
Corrupt men shuddered from good men's fierce swords

Courage was loved more than money
And God's Word - the strength of our land
America, weep for your sins
America, serve God again

Throw your selfishness down
Throw away all your greed
Put your face to the ground
And cry out and plead
Oh, we need mercy
TURN BACK TO GOD, TURN BACK TO GOD
TURN BACK TO GOD

God is wise. He will not continue promoting and blessing a people/nation that is sinning against Him, nor will He demote or curse a people/nation, that is serving Him.

Solomon is quoted saying:

> Diligent hands will rule, but laziness ends in slave labor.
>
> **Proverbs 12:24** (NIV)

What are we, morally diligent or lazy? Each carries a consequence.

> . . . if my people, who are called by my name, will humble themselves and pray and seek my face and turn from their wicked ways, then will I hear from heaven and will forgive their sin and will heal their land.
>
> **2 Chronicles 7:14 (NIV)**

CHAPTER SIXTEEN

✦ ✦ ✦

Responsibility Yields Authority

I want you to carefully read and re-read the following capitalized words.

THE AMOUNT OF RESPONSIBILITY EARNS AN EQUAL MEASURE OF AUTHORITY.

Did you ever notice how the person doing the laundry in the house can be bossy about your dirty laundry? Their responsibility yields authority.

You may have a friend you never take orders from but if he is working on your car and begins asking you to fetch something or hand him tools—you do it.

The one with the responsibility is the one with authority.

It follows the same pattern where Christian involvement is concerned; the less in which Christians get involved, the smaller the circle of our authority, or at the very least, the smaller the circle of our influence.

As Americans gleefully hand over more and more responsibilities to the Federal government, we fail to realize that with the responsibility goes freedom and authority in that area.

As Christians in America continue to sidestep their biblical responsibilities, those that are ungodly are picking up the ball.

Our slack hand will be put to forced labor and the reign of the ungodly will, as always, end in bondage.

The hand of the diligent will rule, but the slack [hand] will be put to forced labor.

Proverbs 12:24 (NASB)

STEWARDSHIP

With great effort many of us have taken principles of stewardship and perverted them in such a way that our conclusion has become "let's not get involved and become worldly". Come again. What is this logic?

It is amazing how much popular teaching has us doing for the church; spending on the church, sending out missionaries, and supporting ministries which is mostly good. But if millions, even billions of dollars were given to me to turn this country around, I could not save this country; neither could more money nor any other Christian man or ministry. We are at the point where the only revival that can save us is individuals understanding his and her need to personally repent of their own sin and error. We must begin to give God the honor He requires in our thoughts, our time, our words, in our actions, and all while fearing Him more than popular opinion. Supporting your church, missionaries, or ministries WILL NOT buy revival—ONLY *your own* REAL REPENTANCE will bring revival.

Your repentance is more valuable to the kingdom of God than your donation.

May God save us from the destruction of deception that is upon us. May He bless our repentance to obedience and effective stewardship. With every opportunity He gives us, we have the opportunity to please Him.

REARRANGING CHURCH EMPHASIS

The church will again have a holy impact on society once its people stop being primarily concerned about fame, attendance numbers, fashion, real estate, and popularity.

What is the priority of your church? Is it to grow in attendance, buy more real estate, upgrade the building, or grow in godliness?

A church should be faithful to God, not merely pleasing to man. The Body of Christ needs once more to promote obedience, faithfulness, honesty, willingness, intelligence, courage, prudence, wisdom, integrity, wholeheartedness, prayer, fasting, and perseverance. We must be honest about where we are falling short and zealously repent.

This is not a self-improvement program or series of talks. We need to be informed and aware of what is happening around us so we can intelligently respond according to God's Will for ourselves and those around us. We need to have the courage to confront error and sin in us and around us, redemptively. We need prudence and wisdom in dealing with these things. We need to have the integrity, wholeheartedness, and perseverance to be involved in spiritual warfare to achieve victory.

Hide or seek? Shall we avoid or shall we overcome?

We need to fellowship with God in prayer, and yes, also in fasting. We simply must emphasize the same things that God emphasizes to be who He wants us to be.

May the Lord deliver us from non-doing teachers. Non-doing teachers reproduce more non-doing teachers.

> Like a lame man's legs that hang limp is a proverb
> in the mouth of a fool.
>
> **Proverbs 26:7 (NIV)**

Godly characteristics can only be reproduced by those who are bearing these traits—these godly characteristics.

If you personally have too few godly qualities, it is within your power to increase the number of qualities and good fruit, but with

God's help. God honors good choices. He doesn't usually make it easy but He does make it worthwhile and promises to never let us get in a situation that is beyond our ability to resist sin. We are NEVER forced to sin.

> No temptation has overtaken you but such as is common to man; and God is faithful, who will not allow you to be tempted beyond what you are able, but with the temptation will provide the way of escape also, that you may be able to endure it.
>
> **1 Corinthians 10:13 (NASB)**

You can say this was a good book, or you can repent and change.

You can now go get another book to read, or you can get on your knees and repent.

You can go watch TV, go about your daily duties, get to your routine, get some food, etc., ***or you can repent for disobeying your wonderful Lord Jesus who has real vision for you.***

You already know the government isn't going to fix the problems in this country. Deep down you know the only hope for our nation is hearts changing, *FOR REAL,* one at a time.

But first, it is time for *your* heart—today.

Persecution will weed out the hypocrites and purify the faithful when it comes but God is willing to purify you now, if you are willing.

My prayer is that we will be comrades in victory and a great joy to our loving Father Who has waited generations for a people that would serve Him uncompromisingly in love.

> But you are a chosen race, a royal priesthood, a holy nation, a people for [God's] own possession, that you may proclaim the excellencies of Him who has called you out of darkness into His marvelous light; for you once were not a people, but now you are the people of God; you had not received mercy, but now you have received mercy.
>
> **1 Peter 2:9-10 (NASB)**

FREEDOM OF EXPRESSION

There is a wonderful premise that truth can prevail in an argument. Lies can make their claims and deceive many, but when all the chips are on the table, those without a secret agenda will see the truth and it will prevail.

There may be another assumption by the founding fathers; that truth is good and worth knowing.

Many in my society hate the truth and instead make arguments based on a much smaller circle of equations. They spit out statistics and draw conclusions from those statistics that are not verifiable and before you can begin to question it, they have not only reached their own conclusion but are condemning all who disagree with them as "anti-good".

A nation with free speech and freedom of the press provides a stage and forum for every nutcase to stand up and start talking. This is OK, because when a rational person stands and speaks truth, the nutcase is exposed as irrational. There are many dishonest people who pretend they are doing good and speaking truth when they are simply manipulating words to achieve their own end. Virtue is in the minority EXCEPT that the young, idealistic, and honest are really interested in the truth. This is a great advantage that speakers of the truth always have. Amidst the crowd of psychos, wackos, liars, manipulators, perverts, and those who are willing to embrace only the words and philosophies that justify their own selfish causes—are the young, idealistic, and honest—hungering for truth. Even if parents, government, or culture have another agenda there are many who are attracted to the best argument. The very best argument is always the truth, if presented correctly.

What a tragedy it is that there are those who know the truth but have stopped arguing. How utterly ruinous it is if the honest and good leave the marketplace, courts, and public forums, to retreat into inner circles where they can safely speak to agreeable listeners. "Amen! Amen!" a chorus of agreement rings out and all are encouraged to return next week to hear some more agreeable words of truth.

America, or more specifically any nation with free speech and elections, is a forum of argument. This is wonderful. Although we are subject to hearing nearly every form of contemptible hogwash served up as "truth" while each group is getting their own "Amens", it is also our opportunity to step forward and reason and argue. I guarantee, the truth will always win new followers and I guarantee those not interested in the truth will only and always disagree. There is nothing new here but this is good news.

Let me put the shoe on the other foot. What if the people in America with every anti-Christian ideology decided they were tired of being criticized and started their own churches? What if they felt their ideas could be shared in a more welcome and dignified setting if they retreated to their own private clubs? What if they got out of our faces and just talked to each other; they stopped lobbying congress, they stopped talking to the media, they stopped voting? That would be great for all of us who oppose them. This would be considered their retreat from the public forum. We would cheer though we would still want them to stop lying, even to each other. After all, they aren't fighting us in the open; they are hiding and criticizing us privately while being self-righteous among themselves.

Sound familiar? This is largely what the American church has done. The very foundation of America, the Bible—God—Christianity—brave and intelligent men and women with admirable morality, honesty, and work ethics have retreated from the absolutely required vigilance of constantly fighting for the truth in an arena of free speech, constant elections, and changing of laws.

With the constant fluctuation of morals, opinions, greed, and agendas to not contend with these is certain surrender. If you are not stepping into the arena to represent you values, your values will simply not be represented.

Truth always has the advantage because truth is always the best argument on a platform of logic and evidence. Truth has no advantage when it is silent. Spiritual battles are never won by soldiers who throw down their swords and go home because of the advancing army against truth.

There are a thousand philosophies, hundreds of religions, and many voices shouting in the streets trying to win the public to their way of thinking. They are selling products, values, lifestyles, habits, sins, heroes, stories, models, envy, lust, versions of success, politics, and answers to every question. Isn't it foolish to try and censor something as wonderful as freedom of speech when it provides the very best opportunity where truth has the advantage.

We must first discover the real truth and see how it holds up to argument. Truth is far more than a war of words. It is living successfully, living with a clear conscience, loving others, and being loyal, trustworthy, and honest in all matters. If we are too busy gathering prosperity for ourselves, too lazy to test the truths we hold dear, or too hypocritical to live what we say we believe—truth is given a bad image. It is the image of you, the believer.

It is so easy to deceive ourselves by flattering one another and trying to believe that we are better than others, but this is not what the Bible teaches.

We benefit from the truth if we abide by the truth.

If we are abiding in the truth and share convincingly the realities of what is always actually true, others benefit. The truth is much broader than the sinner's prayer. Millions are in bondage because they believe any one of a hundred-thousand lies. For them, the truth can set them free. But where is the truth? Who will go and show them?

Lyrics to another of the songs I've written.

WHO WILL GO?

Jesus said we shall really know the truth
The truth will set us free, free indeed
We need to know
We have submitted our lives to the Lord
We've seen the peace, the joy, the love,
A dream coming true
Meanwhile there's people hating, hurting, killing, dying,
crying,
Denying any hope. Is there any hope?

If anyone knows the answer
You should speak up.
These people need to know
And see God work
Who will go? Who will go? Who will go?

We are proclaiming that God loves each and everyone faithfully
On bumper stickers, the radio, in the mail
Scattered tracts on trains and subways—They see no faces.
Where is God's love? They want to know, "Where did it go?"

If anyone knows the answer
You should speak up.
These people need to know
And see God work.
Who will go? Who will go? Who will go?
How else will they know?

Jesus said we shall really know the truth
The truth will set us free, free indeed
We need to know
This generation going down,
They don't know who to blame or whose name to call on
Who can save us?

If anyone knows the answer
You should speak up.
These people need to know
And see God work.
Who will go? Who will go? Who will go?

CHAPTER SEVENTEEN

✦ ✦ ✦

Righteous Leadership

VICTORIES, YOURS AND GOD'S

Victory is the Lord's.

Victory rests with the Lord
Proverbs 21:31 (NIV)

In all the battles that have been fought on this earth, God has never known defeat. God has never lost, as a matter of fact, God OWNS victory. Evil can prevail, but only temporarily. God's people have lost wars but in the Bible it was their sins that got them defeated. The Old Testament shows us this over and over. The faithful within a perverse generation will not be defeated by death because resurrection to eternal reward is far more than religious fluff. It is a promise from the One Who has the superior intellect and power to create life and the universe; a power all men lack.

For you to win a battle against another person, group, or force isn't a decision of yours. It is not based on your strength, speed, allies, or weapons. God is the determining factor because He owns victory.

So how does a person secure victory? In what way can you be more influential in determining the outcome?

The answer: You can decide whether you will be faithful to God. You can seek His Will through study and prayer. The only battle in which you are truly the determining factor is the battle against your own flesh, your own will, YOU.

If you obey God, you win!

Blessed are they whose ways are blameless, who walk according to the law of the Lord. Blessed are they who keep his statutes and seek Him with all their heart. They do nothing wrong; they walk in His ways.

Psalms 119:1-3 (NIV)

"Blessed" can also be accurately translated "happy".

The next time you sense the Holy Spirit requesting something you don't want to give up, open your ear to the trumpet call in the background. This is the battle cry. This is your fight before a great cloud of witnesses.

There is nothing covered that will not be revealed and hidden that will not be known.

Matthew 10:26b (NASB)

There is no glamour or suspense in any battle because God will easily win. The only suspense is when you are deciding whether you will maintain obedience even when to compromise appears to be "sure victory".

Our battlefield is in our will. God's battlefield is everywhere else.

We need to prepare for the battle.

We need to eat well, to consume truth, pure truth.

We need to listen to the true things and be careful to what we submit ourselves.

We need to sharpen our swords, not just carry them.

We need more than to know the truth.

We must train by practicing obeying His Will.

We must be prepared to continue using what we are practicing in *every* arena of life.

We need more than a desire to glorify God; we need to obey Him, and armed with that obedience, enter the arena.

CHRISTIAN CITIZENSHIP

If we are to serve God, there are scriptures that can guide us in our citizenship.

> To do righteousness and justice is desired by the Lord rather than sacrifice.
>
> **Proverbs 21:3 (NASB)**

> Thus says the Lord, "Preserve justice, and do righteousness."
>
> **Isaiah 56:1 (NASB)**

> Learn to do good, seek justice, reprove the ruthless, defend the orphan, plead for the widow...
>
> **Isaiah 1:17 (NASB)**

> Seek good and not evil, that you may live and thus may the Lord God of hosts go with you, just as you have said! Hate evil, love good, and establish justice in the gate!
>
> **Amos 5:14, 15 (NASB)**

We are all growing. If only obedient Bible believers were in office would argument cease? Certainly not, no more would they agree than our own founding fathers that argued for days, weeks, months, and years; but from good men's debating came the creation of our Constitution, the foundation of a very great nation worth preserving in deference to their wisdom.

If God's truth is considered suppressive to many, we need to keep in mind that we are not intruding on someone else's home, hangout, or nation.

This is our country. Satan is the thief, not the owner. God is everyone's Creator whether they believe it or not. God made this world we live in, we are not the intruders. We are not going to be respectful to lies and disrespectful to God anymore.

The right attitude is one of repossessing what is rightfully ours. If the system is still intact we can do it legally using the freedom of expression. The political process and vigilant citizenship is the wonderful power endowed to citizens desiring a voice.

God has given this earth to His people. It is so love and wisdom can reign for the benefit of all people. Our duty is not to merely serve ourselves, but all, as God loves all. As I stated earlier, men died nobly so we could live nobly. Let us claim that inheritance with the perspective that would please Him. The gates of hell shall not prevail against us.

We have but one generation in which to live. This is our generation. We cannot change what has happened before us. Whatever regretful sins we have committed as individuals cannot be changed. We can change today. We can be wiser. Whatever sins we have committed as a people or nation can be acknowledged but the past cannot be changed. Our Christian heritage as a nation also cannot be changed. The history books can be re-written but the reality cannot be changed.

While we have our breath, we can do something here.

If the church does not implement God's values in this country, there is no one else we can wait for to do it. There is great division in American religion. God is not looking for denominations, He is looking for those whom Jesus died for and made right in God's eyes. Jesus died for no organizations but He died for people like us.

If YOU do not personally confront those things that are not of God, there is no one in the church you can blame.

Deliver those who are being taken away to death, and those who are staggering to slaughter, O hold [them] back.

Proverbs 24:11 (NASB)

We cannot wait for the ungodly to popularize righteousness and invite us into the spotlight before we begin to obey God.

David sang of his godly citizens recorded in Psalms.

> Let the high praises of God be in their mouth, and a two-edged sword in their hand, to execute vengeance on the nations, and punishment on the peoples; to bind their kings with chains, and their nobles with fetters of iron; to execute on them the judgement written; This is an honor for all His godly ones.
> Praise the Lord!
>
> **Psalms 149:6-9 (NASB)**

To execute justice is not only a requirement and command of God but a CALLING of God's people and as David declared—an HONOR.

Whose values will dominate our generation, God's, or Satan's? It really is your decision because it already is YOUR generation.

GOD'S CALL

1. Ask God specifically how you are to be involved. Are you to be a voter? Then vote in ALL elections. Vote wisely and know your candidates and the issues.
2. If you are to help certain candidates get elected, what would be YOUR criteria for supporting one?
3. If you are to be a candidate, what shortcomings do you have that God would have you repent of? What would God have you repent to?
4. Ask God for a specific sign to indicate to you exactly what office He wants you to hold.
5. Are there other church members that could help in studying candidates and possibly make this information available to the rest of the church?
6. Write letters to the editor, volunteer at church, become pro-active in community decisions or even new ideas.

7. Work for the weak, the poor, the oppressed, the ill, the lonely—there is absolutely no unemployment in this category.

In addition to doing searches on the internet, you can check for recent listings of useful links at www.ChristiansintheArena.com

There are many arenas: schools, prayer closets, social programs, politics, organizations, etc.

If there is a tug in your heart to address a certain issue or issues, ask God what talents of yours He wants utilized. Who does He want you to work with?

You can donate money but God wants YOU more than your money. Believe it.

May our obedience "be complete". May we show the honor that God deserves by taking everything that He says seriously even if it is contrary to our present way of thinking.

How we need to talk to God about this. Before we talk to anyone else, we must talk to Him about implementing what we now know.

. . . to one who knows [the] right thing to do, and does not do it, to him it is sin.

James 4:17 (NASB)

For though we walk in the flesh, we do not war according to the flesh, for the weapons of our warfare are not of the flesh, but divinely powerful for the destruction of fortresses. We [are] destroying speculations and every lofty thing raised up against the knowledge of God, and we [are] taking every thought captive to the obedience of Christ, and we are ready to punish all disobedience, whenever your obedience is complete.

II Corinthians 10:3-6 (NASB)

> Now all [these] things are from God, who reconciled Himself through Christ, and gave to us the ministry of reconciliation, namely that God was in Christ reconciling the world to Himself, not counting their trespasses against them, and He has committed to us the work of reconciliation. Therefore we are ambassadors for Christ, as though God were entreating through us; we beg you on behalf of Christ, be reconciled to God. He made Him who knew no sin [to be] sin on our behalf, that we might become the righteousness of God in Him.
>
> **2 Corinthians 5:18-21 (NASB)**

There is competition for the spotlight, for leadership, wealth, and approval. However, there is little competition for those willing to serve where there is a need.

Ask God—today.

Obey.

Then ask God daily.

Thank you.

Summary

- You have visualized God's prophets surrendering popularity by proclaiming His truth.
- You know God's call to His people is to proclaim truth, regardless of the moral standards around them.
- You've seen how truth can be despised.
- You read many scriptures condemning ignorance and exhorting us to be knowledgeable.
- You understand that if a godly philosophy doesn't reign in our government an ungodly one will.
- You've learned that law is a minister of God and without Christian people involved in its function, it will be perverted.
- Your own Bible testifies that the righteous should defend the innocent, help the poor, exercise judgment, and destroy wickedness both from positions of leadership as citizens and as servants.
- As His servant, you must discern and proclaim what is right and wrong.

- You have witnessed how God's love has divided, confronted, and offended people through Jesus Christ.
- You realize that tolerance of sin is usually the opposite of merciful.
- You have comprehended that we, the people of God, are experiencing God's judgment just like every generation who forsakes God's Will and spurns Him by their actions.
- You agree we have been poor stewards with our freedom and ability to govern.
- Still, you are certain of God's mighty power with those who are truly repentant.
- You know victory is the Lord's and your only guarantee of being on the victorious side is to win the battle against your own wrong ideas, selfishness, and sins.
- You have clarified in your mind that you are behind enemy lines in this world and this is a time of war with no neutral parties.
- You know God is calling you to repentance.
- You know you must act on His leading.
- Anything you do without love is absolutely not of God and the Bible says it is worthless.

> If I speak with the tongues of men and of angels, but do not have love, I have become a noisy gong or a clanging cymbal. If I have the gift of prophecy, and know all mysteries and all knowledge; and if I have all faith, so as to remove mountains, but do not have love, I am nothing. And if I give all my possessions to feed the poor, and if I surrender my body to be burned, but do not have love, it profits me nothing.
>
> **1 Corinthians 13:1-3 (NASB)**

And it shall come to pass, if thou shalt hearken diligently unto the voice of Jehovah thy God, to observe to do all his commandments which I command thee this day, that Jehovah thy God will set thee on high above all the nations of the earth:

Deuteronomy 28:1 (ASV)

But Peter and the apostles answered, "We must obey God rather than men.

Acts 5:29 (NASB)